## Acknowledgements

We would like to acknowledge Christopher the minister at Colston Milton Parish Church, Milton, Glasgow. The church helped us to find the people who attended our drop in centre, where we were able to witness their transformation and healing, and without them there would be missing chapters. Christine McPherson for her help in editing and Kim and Sinclair for their support to publish the book.

# NOW I UNDERSTAND

## A GUIDE TO LIFE IN LAYMAN'S TERMS

## GERARD MURPHY & LORRAINE BUCHANAN

CAIRNGORM
BOOKS

Published in 2018 by Cairngorm Books

ISBN Paperback: 978-1-9993517-0-0
Ebook: 978-1-9993517-1-7

Published with the help of Indie Authors World
indieauthorsworld.com

IndieAuthors
World

# Dedication

We would like to dedicate the book to our families and everyone we have met over the years, who became the motivation and inspiration behind writing this book.

# Introduction

The reason for writing this book is to help other people who, like me, find change very difficult. Having no self-worth or confidence, I wore a mask most of my life but didn't know why. I don't blame my parents or my environment for the way I turned out, although I did for most of my life. I never once thought I would say this, but I am truly grateful for the life I had then, for it has turned me into the person I am today. And without it, I wouldn't have been able to write this book with Lorraine. Don't get me wrong here: I hated my life and the world, and I blamed other people and my circumstances for my pain. But as you read through the book, you will realise that it's easier to blame than it is to take responsibility and change.

I tried so hard to change but didn't know how. I read hundreds of books, watched people on YouTube, listened to self-help CDs, spoke to spiritual people, went for counselling... yet still found change so difficult. I even studied counselling and many other approaches that worked with the mind, body, and spirit, but still I couldn't find the peace I craved. I didn't trust myself enough that I could change. I kept telling myself, 'It's too hard' – a word I never use today, as I know now that it was a cop-out for not even trying.

This book has been written without any jargon or any complicated words. I know from my own experience that complicated jargon and words confused and intimidated me when I had no confidence or self-worth, and I ended up resenting the author or whoever who was speaking to me. I felt that they thought they were better than me because they used words I couldn't understand. Today, I know that's not the real reason that I got angry and resentful.

In truth, I loathed myself and felt I was stupid; I was envious of others and felt that they were better than me. I was a 35-year-old recovering drug addict and alcoholic with mental health problems, and couldn't even read or write properly. I had no education or confidence, very low self-worth, no self-esteem, and was a chronic people-pleaser. No wonder I was angry all the time! I was trapped in a body of lies. My mind and its negative thought pattern controlled me to the extent that I believed everything I had told myself, and I did this because I believed it to be normal. Trying to change the negative way you have been thinking for all those years is a tall order, especially when you add in your reactions and moods, your attitudes, and so on. It all just becomes frightening if you have no courage or confidence.

One of the main reasons for writing this book is a genuine belief that when we finally begin to understand ourselves, then we can better understand others. In doing this, it saves us from comparing our standards, or judging, having expectations, and making assumptions. Understanding ourselves brings awareness, joy, and an inner peace and confidence like never before. And when we finally learn about us and why we ended up in such a mess, we can then begin to really love ourselves through changing and breaking our old negative habits.

Knowing this and practising change on a daily basis sets us free from a life of pain and sorrow, and brings us to the joy of realising that we are truly powerful. This book has emerged from tried and tested life experience. The approach Lorraine and I use has been developed from wide personal experience of supporting people living with and suffering from addiction, repeated offending, dysfunctional behaviours, and issues of mental health. The material within the book specifically targets a range of unhelpful thinking and behaviour patterns. These patterns have been identified through working with participants over a significant number of years.

Hopefully, you'll find that the information and advice we give is easy to understand. It aims, firstly, to help the reader to identify their own unhelpful thought processes and behaviours; and secondly, to provide them with direction on how these thoughts and behaviours can be changed in order to improve their quality of life, mental health, and inter-personal relationships.

People are encouraged to take responsibility for their own feelings and behaviour. They are also empowered with the necessary skills to identify, challenge, and change their unhelpful thinking and behaviour patterns. In the past, participants we have worked with have commented that our programme, 'Empowering by Example', has enabled them to really 'see' themselves mirrored in the material, and that this has helped them – perhaps for the first time – to become self-aware and to identify the root of their problems. By becoming aware of the consequences of their own unhelpful thinking and behaviour patterns, many have gone on to learn how to make responsible choices, manage moods, improve their health, control anger, and reduce reliance on prescribed medication and mind-altering drugs, including alcohol. Many have also reported a reduction of stress within their close family unit as just one of the positive outcomes resulting from taking part in the programme Lorraine and I offer.

What you are about to read, my friends, is the story of my life in layman's terms – a journey from a life of hurt, pain, and darkness, into a life of peace, serenity, and light. Lorraine and I have worked with people from all walks of life, all ages and cultures, and all in need of support from what life throws at us. But during this time, we got to know ourselves– and for that we are truly grateful. I was a hypocrite for years; someone who had all these qualifications and was expected by society to help, support, and guide others, when really I couldn't support or guide myself. I had never been taught how to deal with my feelings and emotions, or how to change my habitual behaviours, negative thinking, and reactions. Pain was my teacher, but Lorraine, who co-wrote this book, showed me the things which prevented me from changing, and taught me how to change.

We *can* change when we know *how* to change; we *can* be happy. My own life experience and listening to other people's experiences for over 23 years has helped to put this book together. We can only hope you find the identification you have longed for, and which will take you from that dark, dark place you thought was home, back into the light where you belong.

# LET'S GET STARTED

As I mentioned at the beginning, honesty is the key. No matter what emotions you experience whilst reading this book, you were meant to feel them. For the only way for us to change is by admitting to ourselves that we never knew any better, and that our way of thinking and behaving was learned within our own homes and environments. There is no need to feel sad or bad any more; this is the last time you ever need to feel fear, shame, guilt, sadness, and regret. When we finally decide we have had enough and learn to forgive ourselves and change the negative way we think and behave towards ourselves and others, then the pain leaves us. It's quite simple: if you are not doing what you used to do, then there's no need for you to feel the way you used to feel.

Never allow your own thoughts to hurt you, and never allow them to keep you trapped in the past. Instead, deal with your past now, learn from it, and you will have a brighter future. It's insanity to continue to punish yourself for the mistakes you made in the past. But if you learn from them and take responsibility for them, that's amazing progress. And that's the beginning of change.

Take your time reading and working through the book. This is not a race. Just remember, it took years to learn to be insecure, so it takes time to change and break these old habits. Be patient, my friends. What you read in these chapters will get you thinking, so please just open your mind and heart and see where that takes you.

I can promise that within a few days, you will feel the changes; and within a few weeks, others will see them.

This is for you. Do it for you. Find the true you.

# Chapter One

## In the beginning

In the beginning, we are all born into different families, with different upbringings, different standards, morals, ethics, values, etc. Some are born into riches, and some poverty; some have both parents, whilst some only have one – others have no parents at all; some children have great childhoods, others have nightmares.

My experience has finally helped me to understand why this happens, and that's only because I surrendered through pain. But as a child, teenager, and even as an adult, these things really annoyed me. I was so resentful and angry that my parents had split up and that I was poor, and this had a massive negative impact upon my life. But now I think differently.

I now firmly believe that every human being has lessons to learn, and the only way to learn these valuable lessons is by admitting to ourselves that some of the negative things we have learned and the way we have learned to treat ourselves and others at times, is wrong. It's painful and it goes against our true self, which shows love and compassion, but how are we to know this if we are not taught it?

As babies and young children, we are innocent to the ways of the world; we haven't a conscience yet. We are born in the light, free from any darkness, materialism, and all those negative thoughts, feelings, emotions, and behaviours. Look into a young child's eyes and you will see pure love and light, and it's even brighter when they smile. We can see this light in some adults, those who have worked from the inside out, gradually coming back to the innocence of the child. But don't forget that we are *all* born in light and love, and are here on earth to learn powerful lessons. And the greatest of all these lessons is love. Unfortunately, our definition of love is what we have learned from our own home and living environment as we grow up.

As babies and small children, if we are fortunate enough to be able to see and hear, we learn by watching and listening to everyone we come into contact with. It's the same at school – we watch, we listen, and we copy by example. Consciously and unconsciously, we are learning each and every day. We learn initially from our teachers at home – our parents, older siblings, and family members, etc. And when we finally begin school, we find more teachers, including our friends. At that age, though, we aren't aware of this. We are totally innocent to what's going on around us. Our world's one big playground and we love it when we get all the attention; our light shines, and our spirit is free.

However, we aren't aware that what we are seeing, hearing, and unconsciously copying then shapes our personalities and characters. The patterns and behaviours that we learn as children will make us or break us, depending on the message we receive from those teachers. The negative way we learned to think, speak, and behave whilst growing up is just one of life's lessons, and our goal is to become aware of these dysfunctional behaviours and hopefully find the courage, faith, and strength to break them so that we may experience our true selves.

Our purpose in life and our true nature is to give and receive love. This is our biggest and greatest lesson, and when we are doing this we feel absolutely amazing, because we are being true to ourselves. It's the negative behaviours we have learned, and the way we have learned to think and react, that prevents us from living a life of love and peace.

Think about what you have read so far. How did you learn to speak and walk, tie your shoelaces, and brush your teeth? How did you learn to read and write? And how did you learn to become a trades-man/woman, road sweeper, musician, doctor, nurse, businessman/woman, or any career? We learned.

We watch what people are doing and listen to what they are saying. And if we want to learn it, then we will copy and then practise it until we become good at it. But children aren't aware that they are learning and copying, because they are doing it on an unconscious level. It's basically learning without knowing we are learning.

That's why it's so difficult for most people to take responsibility. They don't see anything wrong with their behaviour; it's everyone else's fault. Most, if not all, of our negative thinking and behav-iour and the way we deal with our feelings, emotions, and people, is learned from our childhood and teenage life. These learned behav-iours stay with us, and we truly believe them to be normal. Anger, resentment, selfishness, arrogance, pride, worry, fear, shame, guilt, regret, blame, control, greed, laziness, being judgmental, criticising, etc. There are so many negatives that I have lost count.

At the age of about 7 or 8, we begin to gradually lose our inno-cence; for some, it can be taken from them a lot earlier, depend-ing upon their upbringing. Once that innocence is removed, our conscience appears. And as we all know by now, this is something that we can listen to and learn from, or ignore and stay trapped in darkness and pain.

I believe that this is the age at which we should be taught about life. As young children, we are not aware of our negative feelings and emotions, nor the cause and the effect they have on us, on others, and on our wellbeing. We are not aware nor do we understand why we tell lies, why we wet ourselves at home and at school, why we feel bad within, why we feel different from others. Do we understand unhappiness, loneliness, what fear really is and what it can do to us?

Fear is anyone's worst nightmare, never mind for a child experiencing it constantly. Fear is the complete opposite of love, and the main root and cause of most of life's problems. It has caused wars, murders, addictions, severe mental health problems throughout the world, suicides, greed, etc.

But sadly, getting an education in order to earn plenty of money, live the life of Reilly, and keep up with the Jones's, seems more important. It always has and always will be.

If only society could understand that as adults, parents, and carers, we are the only ones who can help to break this cycle of dysfunction, so that our children and their children can have the chance of living a life free from fear and learn to be true to themselves.

As much as children are beautiful and honest, they can also be very cruel, tell lies, and blame others. Something else they learned! I can remember stealing at a very early age, due to the pressure from other children. It was that unknown fear that if I didn't do what I was asked, then I would be laughed at or bullied and, even worse, left on my own with no friends. This pressure caused me to shoplift even though I knew it was wrong. I also stole other people's clothes from washing lines so that I could fit in and be liked. I told lies to impress my peers and behaved like a clown so that I could be a part of the crowd and not left out on my own. As a child, I didn't know any better, but I became more aware of what I was doing at around the age of eight. Yet, at that time, I didn't understand the horrible feelings and emotions which come from not being true to ourselves.

It's only as we get older that we develop a conscience – that loving little voice within us which is there to guide us, which tells us right from wrong, and tries to guide us back to innocence. It's also the voice we learn not to listen to. Later in the book, you will find out why.

What we learn whilst growing up, especially the way we think and behave towards ourselves and others, has a massive impact on how we are going to feel throughout our lives. It's not just those from dysfunctional families and backgrounds we are talking about here. Even children who were raised with proper standards, values, ethics, morals, and bags of love, have ended up in Rehab for drug and alcohol abuse, institutions for their mental health problems, prison, or taken their own lives. If we are not properly taught to understand ourselves and life, and how to recognise and deal with our negative feelings and emotions, then we will simply react and deal with them the way we have learned to react and deal with them.

I can see now that I wanted to fit in as a child because of my unconscious fears and insecurities. I wanted to be liked and I wanted attention. I began to tell lies, to worry, feel fear, shame, guilt, loneliness, anger, resentment, and many more negative feelings and emotions, and I didn't have a clue what was happening to me. When my parents split up, I was just five years of age, and I believe this is when the hurt really began. There wasn't much love within our home after that; plenty of anger and fights, but not much love. My dad, bless him, tried his best. He had to leave his job to take care of us all, which was very difficult back in the 1960s. He had no money and must have been hurting pretty badly because, as much as he loved us and tried his best, he became very angry at times. All of this happened, and happens, because most parents and people don't know what love really is.

They don't understand or are aware that what they have learned is a habit, so they believe it to be ok for them to be angry and in pain all the time. It's normal for them, but it doesn't mean they don't love us. They're only doing what *they* learned to do and, if we are honest, loving ourselves is very, very difficult at times. Most parents also fall into the trap of thinking that spoiling children with material items and giving them what they want is showing love.

Children crave attention and all they want to do is to play and have fun; how easy we forget this as adults. We forget because of what we have gone on to learn as we grew up, and we have allowed the pressures of life to control us, i.e., relationships, careers or being famous, money and the love of it, drugs, alcohol, sex, crime, and basically anything that takes us away from being true to ourselves.

Some of the behaviours we have learnt whilst growing up are the things that keep us trapped in pain. Fear of other people and what they think of us; the way we think and speak about others; jealousy and envy of what others have that we don't have; telling lies and seeking approval, etc.

The insecurities we learned whilst growing up are the same ones our parents learned from their parents and their environments; they're passed down from one generation to the next. So, please try and understand this important point and don't be too hard on yourself. Through this understanding, you can find some peace and maybe even forgiveness.

Remember when you were an innocent child, and you would look people in the eye and tell them the truth that you didn't like them? Not once did you think about how they would react; you never did their thinking for them. It's important to keep thinking about that time of childhood innocence, as it helps us to understand and recognise why we are unhappy and in pain, and why we are always chasing and searching for people, places, things, and situations to make us happy. If we can't understand that, then we will stay trapped in that life which we have so far believed to be normal.

Think back to when you started school or nursery, and you were about to paint your first picture. Now, this isn't just any picture. This is a picture every child paints; a picture we carry with us our whole entire lives, believing that if we have what is in this picture we will be happy. Again, unconsciously, we learn this as children and nobody tells us any different, because we are all chasing the same picture.

If you can't remember painting this picture yourself, then I'm pretty sure you have seen your own children or other children painting it. Do you know the one I mean? The sun is shining with a smile on its face, or maybe even a rainbow in the background; there's the big house with the picket fence; the car in the driveway and the lovely garden with the flowers; you, and maybe your brother or sister, are holding hands with Mummy and Daddy, and all of you are smiling. Do you remember it now? Usually Mummy or Daddy will proudly put it on the wall or on the fridge, for everyone to see.

Most people throughout the world will chase and search their entire lives for this picture, believing that when they get it, they will have true happiness and peace. When we painted it – all those years ago – everyone was smiling and happy, including the sun and the flowers.

But it's an illusion, my friends. And one which brings unbelievable pain, heartache, bankruptcy, divorce, families torn apart, crime, addictions, suicide, and death.

That was to be my life whilst growing up within my environment. I chased this picture and believed that money, people, and material things, would make me happy. I began to steal money when I was around ten years old, because I felt better when I had money. I didn't feel like a tramp or a poor person any more; I felt good about myself. So good that I continued with that kind of behaviour until I was 35 years of age! I went chasing and searching for people, places, and things to make me happy, because I didn't know that what I was doing was wrong. I went through my life blaming everyone else for my own pain... because of what I had learned.

My conscience was trying to guide me but I didn't like hearing the truth, so I chose to listen to my ego instead, which is the voice of lies. Severe emotional pain, numerous suicide attempts, and addiction, helped me to become honest and to change.

We hope that never happens to anyone. We hope you gain the awareness and understanding you need in order for you to begin the process of change.

**Let's recap:**

This first chapter is important in opening your mind a little and helping you to understand:

✦ what happens to us at the beginning of our journey

✦ how we learned what we know by unconsciously learning from others

✦ how not knowing or understanding what was happening to us, we went searching for love in the wrong places

So, now we need to have a look at some of the predicaments we find ourselves in, the insecurities and negative behaviours we have learned whilst growing up, and also this picture of happiness we have unconsciously created and chase.

# Chapter Two

## What we learned

Try to remember, my friends: we never left our mother's wombs with all these negative behaviours and insecurities. We learned them over a period of time, and for most people they are very difficult to break. I'm not saying you can't break them. What I am saying is that we have been doing them for so long now that the behaviours are habitual – and it's a true saying, old habits die hard. But with awareness, honesty, courage, and understanding, we really can change.

When we were young children and we didn't get our own way, we would throw a tantrum, scream and shout, and stamp our feet, but minutes later we would be back playing with our toys as if nothing had happened.

But as we get older, these tantrums can turn into full blown anger and rage, resentment and hatred, and in some cases even violence – and all because we can't get what we want. If we are behaving like this towards our own family, the people we say we love and would do anything for, then obviously our definition of love is wrong. As a child you would say sorry and look for a cuddle or a kiss to make up for your bad behaviour, but as we get older and leave that innocence behind, we become selfish, inconsiderate, and disrespectful. I can understand this, especially if you were raised within a dysfunctional home and treated badly, but what about those of you who believe they had a very good upbringing? Why do you speak and behave aggressively towards your parents, family, and friends? Can you answer this without justification and blame?

This is a journey of self-discovery, and it takes time, honesty, and courage. But most of all, you need to have an open mind to be able to finally realise that all the negative things we have learned are there for a reason. We are here on this earth to learn; our souls have a purpose, and that purpose is to give and receive love. This is our job, and we all know deep down that when we are being kind and showing compassion and love to ourselves and others, we reap the benefits. What we give is what we receive, and how we think is how we will feel.

So, let's enter into the unknown and take a look at all the negative behaviours we learned and copied unconsciously whilst watching and listening as innocent children. I am giving you a few examples to consider, and I hope and pray you can open your mind and heart and try to look for the similarities and not the differences. Our upbringings may differ but we all have feelings and emotions, and unless we understand what happened to us and how to recognise and change these negative behaviours, then we will always struggle and remain in pain.

We learned how to behave, how to deal with the issues that we face in life, how to conduct relationships, and how to communicate our feelings, from the role models in our lives, i.e. our parents, siblings, peers, and surrounding environment. We're not aware that the way we choose to conduct ourselves is how we have seen our role models conduct themselves throughout their lives.

Here are a few examples of some learned behaviours, the unknown habits we have formed, and the pain which comes from not knowing or understanding.

## Dealing with issues

When we are faced with different issues in our lives, we deal with them in the way our parents, siblings, and peers dealt with similar issues. If we are truly being honest with ourselves, we repeat patterns of behaviour which we swore at one time or another we would never repeat.

The issues that cause us fear and anxiety will be very similar to the same issues that caused our parents fear and anxiety. For example, if our parents worried about financial problems, we also learn to worry when faced with financial problems. If our parents did not act responsibly when it came to paying bills, then most likely we will be the same.

So, put simply, if we have not been influenced in a positive, spiritual, and responsible manner by a family member or friend, then we can only play with the cards we have been dealt.

You will also see that the demands we make on our children will be similar to the demands that were made on us, even though at some point in our lives we swore we would not treat our children in the same way! We also find ourselves trying to enforce the same rules that we lived by as children, i.e. 'I didn't get that at your age, and I wasn't allowed to do that, so you're not allowed to do that.' But the reason we enforce these rules is that, without thinking, we are behaving in the only way we know how; the way we learned to. It's the same when we are worried about something; we mirror how one of our parents acted in similar situations. If they paced the floor when they were anxious, for example, then we will pace the floor when we are anxious.

We all have behaviours that mirror another member of our family. In fact, you'll notice that we even point it out to others at times – 'You are just the same as your father/mother/brother/sister.' We not only look and sound like our parents and siblings, but we behave in a similar manner –some good, some bad. When someone says that we are just like our parents, they don't always mean that we *look* like them. Often it can be because we have the same way of dealing with issues, the same actions, the way we walk, our body language, the way that we act and react. Remember, unconsciously, as children we watched, listened, and copied. How else did we learn?

## Putting conditions on others

Most of us have learned that to be nice to other people, they must meet our conditions. And basically, conditions are prejudices. Prejudices are not just about the colour of your skin, or what religion you are, or what football team you support.

There are all sorts of conditions that others must meet for us to approve of them. The way that others speak, for instance, or where they live, how they dress, if they're of the same opinion as us, or if they have more money than we do or more qualifications. There are so many conditions that we put on others before we will offer them our friendship. And if we haven't learned to respect others simply for who they are, then we will treat them with contempt if they are not the same as us. We measure other people by the standards that we set for ourselves, because we are not comfortable with anyone that appears to be different from us.

We sometimes see a mirror of our negative side in other people, which can cause us to become angry and judgmental with them. But we don't realise we are doing these things. We are not aware that it's not the other person's fault that we don't feel comfortable with them; it's just the way we have learned to behave, and we believe that what we are doing is normal.

## Blame

When we apportion blame, we are not taking responsibility for our actions. We are too busy going over and over in our minds trying to find a reason why *we* are not to blame. It's perfectly natural to blame something or someone else when things don't go the way we want them to or when something goes wrong. When we have done something wrong or we have had an accident of some kind, we blame because we are afraid of the consequences of our actions; we fear how other people are going to respond to us, and the shame that we will bring upon ourselves or our family. Added to that is the fear of others finding out what we have done and knowing that they are going to be talking about us.

Most of us are not encouraged to take responsibility for the behaviours which we see in our environment; we think that admitting we made a mistake is going to get us into trouble, even when our wrong-doing was accidental.

We are so afraid of feeling shame and inferior that we have to find an excuse for what we have done, hoping and praying that it will get us off the hook. So we learn how to make excuses for what we have done, and find someone or something else to blame. We blame others for our own guilt, then later feel guilty for allowing someone else to take the blame for us.

We have watched and listened to our parents, siblings, friends, and members of our environment do exactly the same thing – they make excuses and find reasons why they were not responsible for what they have done. It works for them, so we do the same thing – it's normal. Even something as simple as knocking over or dropping a favourite vase in the house – we find a reason for how the accident happened: 'Who left that lying there? If they had been looking where they were going… It wasn't just my fault…'

And we don't just blame others when we are in trouble. We also blame them when we don't want to do something – for example, 'My mum won't let me; I am not allowed out; I can't make it because the babysitter let me down; sorry, I have to work late; I can't afford to go out.' We find something or someone else to blame instead of just telling the truth.

It's also natural to look to others when we are making decisions, and to ask others for advice. But when we take that advice, what happens when things don't go the way that we want them to, or EXPECT them to? We blame our advisors. Of course, we don't tell them that we blame them or that we are angry with them; we just blame them. We justify the truth and begin to think, 'If only I hadn't listened to them, then I wouldn't be in this situation.'

We have learned over the years not to be responsible for our actions, and that to blame someone else is normal: 'If they hadn't done that; if they hadn't said that; everyone else was doing it, etc.'

We do not want to look at the consequences of our actions. We do not want to feel the shame and guilt. We do not want to admit that we are responsible for our own actions. It is so much easier just to blame others than it is to face the consequences of our actions and become responsible.

### Jealousy

We learn to be envious and to be jealous of others.

Jealousy is quite simply to want what someone else has. If we had what they had, we would not be feeling the way we do; they have something that we think would make us feel better if we had it.

Envy is the feeling of anger or dislike that we feel towards another person for the way that they look, how popular they are with other people, the type of person that they are.

Sometimes we are jealous because someone has more money than we do, they live in a bigger house, a nicer area, have better clothes than we do, are receiving more attention than we are. It's the same when we see other people getting something and we don't; we hurt inside and we feel left out. We are afraid that we are not loved any more. And when we compare ourselves to other people and wish that we were like them, it means that we don't like ourselves.

When our parents, partner, or friends pay more attention to someone else, we can also begin to feel inferior. We worry that this other person is liked more than we are, and if we are honest, it's the attention being given to the other person that causes the jealousy… and fear. Fear that the other person is better than us, and that our partner or loved ones will want to spend more time with them and less with us.

You will see these situations played out every day and in every family. There is always someone who has the latest trends and fashions; the neighbour who has the newest, fanciest car; the brother or sister who try to always have something better than their siblings. We can feel this way about any human being; we can even become jealous of our own children.

But when we feel jealous of other people or what they have, it's really because we are not happy within – and what we are really feeling is threatened. Quite simply, we are afraid that they will receive more attention than us.

## Shame

Shame is a feeling aroused by having done something or not done something, said something or not said something. And when we live like this, it creates shame and guilt. It's the same when we become embarrassed and ashamed by other people's behaviour – some time later, we will feel guilty and ashamed for thinking like that.

But we have learned to feel ashamed by the role models in our lives. Over the years, parents, teachers, friends, religious teachers, employers, etc, have probably told us when we have done something wrong that we should be ashamed of ourselves, that we should know better. I'm sure we've all heard 'Don't you realise that you are ruining the good name of the family/school/church?'

There are also times that we feel ashamed of the behaviours of our parents and the rest of our family, because we know this is not the way we would choose to conduct ourselves. We might be ashamed of the way our parents behave, the condition of our home, the way that our parents and siblings have acted towards us, and even the way that they dress.

But this is not our shame to feel, my friends. You are not them. We are not responsible for the way that other people choose to think and behave.

As children, we might have felt ashamed of the condition of our home, the state of our clothes, the way that we dressed, our lack of money. We were perhaps ashamed of our parents and the way that they acted towards each other, towards us, the way they chose to conduct themselves. But just because we are related to or friends with someone, it does not mean that we have to live up to their expectations or to the same rules and morals as they do; it does not mean that we have to feel what they should be feeling. We are not responsible for the behaviours of others, so why do we feel the shame when it is not our shame to feel?

We feel the shame because we are afraid of what others will think of us.

But the only time we should feel shame is when *we* are responsible for what we are feeling ashamed of. We are not responsible for other people's behaviours, either in the past or the present. The only person that you are responsible for is yourself.

## Honesty

When we have lived in an environment where it is normal to be dishonest, we learn that it is acceptable to be dishonest. If we have been encouraged to tell lies to cover for other people in our environment, we learn to cover for others without a second thought, i.e. 'Don't tell your mother; don't tell your father; if that's for me, I'm not in; cover for me, tell my mum I was at yours last night; you haven't seen me; please don't tell them, you know what will happen if they find out.' We tell lies for others because we don't like to see other people getting into trouble, so we cover for them. We cover for them because we want to be liked by them.

We also lie sometimes because we have been threatened; perhaps we have been told what will happen to us if we open our mouths. We know that if we tell, and others find out it was us, we will be talked about, or called names, or bullied and shunned by others. Other times, we lie because we feel that we don't really have a choice; we know that if we were to say something, someone could end up in big trouble. At first, it might just be a little white lie that we are telling – nothing to worry about, nobody is getting hurt.

But when we choose to lie for other people, what happens is that one day we can find ourselves telling lies that make us feel really uncomfortable.

We might even find ourselves in a position where we are telling lies to someone in authority. And if this is the case, we will spend many nights worrying about getting caught.

If we have lived in an environment where goods are stolen, where a member of our family steals, we can easily believe that stealing is normal. So we won't think twice about taking something that does not belong to us, or taking something and not paying for it, because that will feel like normal behaviour.

Being honest with ourselves is about being genuine, truthful, and meaning what you say – not just saying it for the sake of keeping someone else happy. Many of us grew up seeing the adults and role models in our lives telling lies to each other, and expecting others to cover for them – including us. So we learned that it was okay to tell lies to others, it's assumed that we will agree, and it doesn't matter who we are covering for. We even tell lies ourselves and ask others to cover for us; it's often a way of life; it's normal.

Let's see if you can identify with any of these 'little white lies':

If so-and-so phones, tell them I am in the bath.

Just say that I am sleeping.

Don't mention how much that cost in front of your father.

If my girl/ boyfriend phones, don't tell them where I am going.

You haven't seen me.

Don't tell my mum/dad.

Sound familiar? We learn to tell lies from an early age, and we learn that it will stop us from getting into trouble. We know that to tell lies for another person means we are stopping them from getting into trouble, too. So we believe it's alright to tell lies if it means that we and others don't have to face the consequences of our actions.

But, as we all know by now, that isn't true. Your conscience, which is your guide and the truth, will always tell you when you have gone against your true self.

## Gossip

Talking about other people – whether it is good or bad – and whilst they are not present, is carrying stories, tales, or gossip. Gossiping about other people and things that are none of our business is another learned behaviour. It is something that we have all done at some time or another. None of us likes to believe that we gossip, but it's something that is found in all areas of society – at home, work, and in social environments. It is normal for people to talk about each other; it gives them something to talk about and makes them feel important. And if we have something to say or something to talk about, we feel accepted by others taking part in the conversation. It helps us to attract attention, especially where there is a group of people and everyone is struggling to feel as if they belong. In many cases, the character of the person who is being talked about is blackened, or their private business is being discussed, or their morals and standards are being questioned, and all because they are different from the person who has started the gossip.

Gossips feel important, as if they fit in, as if they belong. It helps to reassure them that they are right and the other person is wrong.

But when we have taken part in gossip, we often find ourselves worrying sometime later about what we said. We know that what we did was wrong, and as a result we feel guilty and ashamed, because we wouldn't like to think people were talking about us in the same way. That feeling of guilt can be so strong that, if there were only two of us gossiping, we can find ourselves phoning the other person and asking them not to repeat what we said.

## Communicating our feelings: Anger

The expectations we put onto others, like expecting them to live their lives as we do, are massive within society. And when other people don't live up to our expectations or standards, we become disappointed and angry with them.

We learn how to communicate what we are feeling and how to show our anger in the same way as one or both of our parents did. And there are many ways to show our displeasure when we are not getting our own way:

+ Some of us will start off by shouting; we might slam doors; stamp our feet; go into a huff; not speak to anyone until we finally realise that it doesn't matter, we are still not getting our own way.

+ Some people have learned to communicate their feelings by crying uncontrollably, thinking that their sobbing will get them their own way.

+ Some of us will even threaten, while others resort to violence, depending on how we have learned to show our anger.

+ Some of us will be so angry that our bodies and nervous systems will suffer dramatically.

But we are not born violent or angry; we learn to be violent and angry in the same as we learn to justify our behaviour. We have this false belief that it is only children who throw temper tantrums, but it's adults who teach the children how to throw a tantrum. Children learn everything they know from what is happening in their environment.

## Respect

Respect is when we treat others with consideration, when we are polite to them, when we admire them, and when we are showing love. But if we have lived and socialised in an environment where there has been conflict and no respect shown to one another, we learn that it is normal to be disrespectful.

We see people treating others in our environment with contempt; we see it in the newspapers, in magazines, and on the TV. And if our parents and the adults in our environment have regularly been in conflict with one another, numerous types of behaviours will have been displayed which have become normal to us.

Perhaps there has been name-calling during conflict, so we learn that it is alright for us to call others names and to allow others to call us names.

It's alright to make faces and scowl, to make gestures with our fingers and our hands, to talk to others in a tone that they will feel humiliated by. We feel it's ok to ignore someone because we do not like what is being said, or we don't want to do what we are being asked to do, or –the daddy of them all – because we don't like to hear the truth about ourselves.

How we learn to treat others is the same way that we will allow others to treat us, because we don't see anything wrong with it.

However, respect for another person is treating them in a polite and considerate manner, no matter how different their views are from ours. Respect is recognising that although someone appears to be different on the outside, they still have feelings on the inside. No matter our creed, colour, religion, sex, or social standing, we all experience the same feelings; we all hurt when we are not being shown the respect we deserve as a person.

## Telling lies to impress

There is another reason that we tell lies, and that's to impress others. We often tell lies about our age, our marital status, where we live, or what kind of a job we have. We might tell stories about places we have been, people that we have met, people that we know, and situations that we have found ourselves in. Often it's because we feel we have nothing else to say, so we lie because of the way we feel about ourselves, and it means we receive the attention that we crave.

In many cases, the area that we live in, the amount of money that we have, and what our parents do for a living, can cause us to feel ashamed of our background. So we lie, because we imagine that the truth would mean we would not be accepted in the company we are in.

When a member of the opposite sex catches our eye, we forget to mention that we are with someone and have children; some people might even remove their wedding ring. While it is normal to find ourselves attracted to people other than our partner – the ego loves it, and it's part of human nature – we all know that once we have started the lie, we have to carry on with our pretence, telling more and more lies.

This behaviour of always being out to impress is a result of not knowing how to love ourselves and to be truthful to others.

## Lies to be spiteful

We can also tell lies to get someone we are angry with into trouble. It could be because we want revenge, or we don't like them, or think that they deserve it. We often lie when someone has treated us badly. We might decide to seek our revenge by telling people things that are not true about the other person, either getting them into trouble with someone from authority, or with their family, friends, and members of their environment.

We want them to hurt the same way that we did, and blaming and lying is a normal pattern of behaviour now. But we are completely unaware that what we give out is what we get back, and the way that we think is the way we feel.

So the only person that hurts when we are being spiteful and dishonest, my friends, is us.

## Trust

Trusting in another person is to believe in them without investigating them. The basis of any relationship is trust and honesty, no matter who the relationship is with – parents, partner, friends, or children. When we live in an environment where others have been dishonest with each other, we learn to become suspicious of others.

Perhaps we were treated with suspicion as children and teenagers, being asked question after question: 'Where have you been? Who have you been with? What time did you go there? What time did you get in at?' So, over time we also learn to be suspicious of others and their motives. We already know that we tell lies for others and that others tell lies for us. When we become suspicious, we will go to any lengths to prove that we are right not to believe what we have been told. We replay every word, every action, over and over in our minds, making sure that everything fits in.

We listen to everything that is being said and ask a series of questions, in the hope that our suspicions will be confirmed.

It's natural that if we've been lied to in previous relationships, we will find it hard to trust others. But when there is no trust, there will be inner conflict, and we then become afraid to talk to the other person and to be honest with them. There is a fear that we are wrong, or a fear that we are right which will lead to us having to make a decision that we don't want to make.

When we don't trust other people, we often also learn not to trust ourselves. Trust is something that we should not just give to other people because they seem nice. It is something that is earned over a period of time, through getting to know and accepting that person for who they are… ourselves included.

## Love

We learn about the word love, and how to show our love for others, from the environment where we have lived. For example, if we are from a family where love is shown by touch, we also learn to give a kiss or a cuddle; it is what we have witnessed happening throughout our life.

If we were going out and were told 'I love you', or at the end of a telephone conversation we tell the other person that we love them, then this is the way that we will choose to let our children and partner know that we love them.

If we lived in an environment where our parents showed their love by the gifts and presents they gave us, then this is how we will show our love to our partner and children, and this is how we will measure another's love for us.

Our emotional hurt and pain is there to teach us that when we are hurting, we are not loving ourselves. And this is down to our own definition of love.

Our definition of love is full of expectations – pictures, learned behaviours, and pain, which caused us to loathe, hate, and despise ourselves and others. If we constantly seek approval and love from others, we need to change how we think, because these kind of thoughts are very damaging and prevent us from receiving all the love, teachings, and healing we need in order for us to change, mature, and to love unconditionally.

Nearly every human being will have their own definition of love as a result of their own upbringing, their faith, their own personal beliefs, or whatever they have read or experienced. But one thing we can be sure of is that if we are always looking for others to love us, it's because of our horrible past and what happened to us, the way we have learned to think, and simply not knowing how to love ourselves.

It takes a heck of a lot of pain and sorrow to find out the true meaning of love... but we do get there, my friends. Because, with honesty and courage – two virtues that lie within every single one of us – anything is possible, especially when we desire to be free from pain.

Yet before we experience unconditional love, we have to understand what it is that's preventing us from receiving it. And hopefully, the next chapter should really help with that.

## Let's recap:

In this chapter, we have discussed certain types of learned behaviours and fears, which can be detrimental for our growth. Hopefully, the examples shown will have increased your awareness and helped you to understand why you do what you do and why you feel how you feel.

# Chapter Three

## Pressure, seeking and pleasing

Do you remember your adolescence, your teenage life? Or would you rather forget it? Here are a few examples that might trigger a few laughs or a few tears.

We live in a society where peer pressure is common. It is not just something we have to deal with in our youth; it can rear its ugly head throughout our life. Peer pressure is when we join in with whatever the rest of the company is doing. Peer pressure is doing whatever is being asked simply because we do not want to bring attention to ourselves. We all know what it is like when we are made the centre of attention; most of us don't like it when everyone is watching us.

As a result, we can end up agreeing with something that we don't really agree with, or doing something that we don't want to. But we know deep down that if we decide not to do whatever everyone else is doing, we will either be humiliated, called names, or made to look stupid by others, and then everyone will be talking about us. Basically, peer pressure is a form of bullying that can start when we are very young, but unconsciously we carry it with us into our adult life.

### Peer pressure in adolescence

When we are teenagers, there is a need to be the same as everyone else. If we are not the same, or dare to be different from the crowd, we will probably have to put up with name-calling from others.

When we are with a group of people, there is always someone who will have a 'good idea' and expect everyone else to join in. It could be underage drinking, taking drugs, bullying one particular member of the group, vandalism, or shoplifting.

Even though we know it's wrong or we feel uncomfortable taking part, we can feel the pressure, the horrible feelings in our stomach, and the fear of being singled out if we don't. So we just go along with whatever it is. We don't think of the consequences of our actions; we only think of the fear of being singled out if we don't take part.

It even involves simple things like having the same style of clothes, the same brand of trainers. We have to have what is considered to be the 'in thing', because if we don't, again we might bring attention to ourselves. We don't want to go out and meet our friends and be laughed at because our clothes and shoes are not the latest fashion; we want to feel as if we belong.

No teenager wants to be on their own. We all want to be part of the crowd; we want to be popular; we want to have people to hang around with and somewhere to hang around. But at that age we don't realise that we are more afraid of what our friends think of us than the views of our parents and others in authority.

We don't think about the consequences of our actions and how they could easily have an effect on the rest of our life. Yet it only takes one person to have a really positive idea, and that good idea could be to go against the crowd. Not everyone in the group wants to do whatever it is that is being suggested; it's just that they are all afraid to go against the one who has the most to say – in other words, the bully.

And there is *always* a bully. Yet what we don't realise is that they are the ones who are the most afraid out of the whole group. They are the ones who need everyone to be copying or doing whatever it is that they are suggesting. Why? Because *they* are afraid of being bullied; *they* are the ones who are making sure that it is not them who feel the fear; they don't want people knowing that really deep down *they* are afraid.

## Peer pressure in adult life

Think that peer pressure is something that only happens to us when we are teenagers? Wrong, my friends. It starts as peer pressure when we are young, and becomes people-pleasing when we become adults.

No matter our age, we all find ourselves in situations where we are afraid to do what we really want to do because other people will talk about us and we will become the centre of attention. We are afraid that suddenly all eyes will be on us because we have chosen not to do what everyone else is doing.

For example, we are in the pub with our friends and decide it is time to go home, but there is always someone who will bring to the attention of everyone else that we are about to leave. We know that we should be going home, but suddenly all eyes are on us... and the teasing begins: 'Just stay for another; one for the road; the night is young; running home to Mummy?; your partner got you under the thumb?'

None of your friends is stopping to consider that you might actually want to go home, that there is something else that you would rather be doing. They don't see this, and because they're enjoying themselves they don't see anything wrong with what they are saying.

And it's the fear of them talking about us that convinces us to stay. Why? Because we have to be one of the boys or one of the girls; we don't want to be different; we want to be the same as everyone else.

Or, you're visiting a friend, and as it gets nearer the time that you have planned to leave, another friend calls in. 'Oh, don't go! It's ages since we have seen each other,' they urge. 'Sit down and have another tea/coffee. You don't really need to go just now, do you?' As a result, you feel as if you can't say no, and find yourself still sitting there an hour after you had planned to leave.

It might sound amusing now, but not at the time. When we are with our friends and other people, we are often frightened of what they are going to think and say about us. But we never stop to think about how *we* are going to feel after we have been roped into doing something we didn't want to do. Sometimes that fear of losing face in front of our friends can even cause us to fall out with our partners or parents.

We create an image of ourselves to our friends – an image which they would approve of. But we aren't really showing them our true colours. And, of course, when we have created that image, we have to live up to it… no matter the consequences. Then we become frightened to change our behaviour because our friends might not like us any more; they might not think that we are a good laugh, or that we are going soft.

If we continue to bow to this pressure, without even realising it, it can lead us into all sorts of problems. It could affect our chances of employment; see us being thrown out of the house; getting a criminal record; becoming dependent on drugs/alcohol, mentally ill, or even suicidal. And this all happens because we wanted to be part of the gang, one of the boys or girls, and because we didn't have the courage to just say NO.

Hopefully these next few pages will really open your mind and help you with the understanding and awareness you need in order to realise what prevents us from loving ourselves.

## Self-seeking behaviours

What are self-seeking behaviours? They are behaviours we use to seek praise from other people and to help us feel good about ourselves. Don't get me wrong, it's natural to want to feel good about ourselves; we all like to be patted on the back and told what a good job we have done and how clever we are. We want people to think, 'Oh, what a nice person that is. They would never do you a bad turn.' Or when someone says, 'I don't know what I would have done without you.'

When we help other people in whatever way we can, it gives us a boost. We feel needed, and it makes us feel important. When others are praising us and smiling at us, showing their admiration or giving us a hug, we feel their love, we see their love, and we hear their love.

But if we are not aware of their love, then it is their scorn that we will be aware of. And when we are aware of other people's scorn, we either become defensive or we do our best to please the other person.

If we become defensive, there will no doubt be a battle for control in the relationship. When there is a battle for control, there will always be conflict. And engaging in conflict is when we gradually begin to lose control of ourselves. We feel bad and we feel guilty, because we know deep down that we have done something wrong. We know that we have done wrong, whether the other person else started it or not, and we dislike ourselves. Those horrible feelings – stomach churning, head bursting, nerves going, and the knowledge that in some way we have let ourselves down.

No-one wants to feel like that, my friends. We want to feel good, we want to feel liked, and we want to feel loved. We want to feel as if we fit in somewhere, as if we belong. When we feel as if we belong, we are comfortable with ourselves and with others. It's our fear of the feelings which conflict creates that all too often sees us looking to others for the love we should feel for ourselves, and that's why we seek our happiness in other people.

## How we seek approval

As children, we learn to recognise love when we are smiled at, given praise, shown admiration, or given a kiss or a cuddle. When we experience these, we feel approved of and accepted, we feel comfortable with ourselves and with the people around us. But as we get older, unfortunately we believe that we need to be shown these conditions in order to approve of ourselves, to love ourselves, and to feel good about ourselves.

## Our need

Needing to see a smile on the faces of others to allow us to feel good about ourselves, can find us giving our lives away to other people. This need to please others can find us buying things that we don't want to buy or cannot afford, going places that we don't want to go, and being in company that we don't want to be in. It also leads to us doing what other people want us to do instead of doing what *we* want to do, and the feelings created through not being true to ourselves can be crippling. Here are a few more examples which may help with your awareness and understanding as to why we do this:

*Take the teenager whose parents are at work, who then has somewhere to invite their friends when it is cold outside. They feel needed, they feel important, and they never think about the consequences of their actions.*

*The driver who ends up offering to ferry everyone about, even though they were not going in that direction. And now that they have started doing this, they feel obliged to keep doing it, despite their inner feelings of anger and resentment.*

*The child who chooses a career because Mummy and Daddy think that their choice of career will make them proud. They feel that for Mummy and Daddy to love them, they must do as their parents say, but they are unhappy and continue to be unhappy just to please other people.*

*The people who talk and talk. It doesn't matter what they are saying or who they are talking about. So long as someone is listening to them, they feel important. They hear approval when they are engaged in conversation, so it makes them feel good about themselves.*

*The parents who can never say no to their child, regardless of their age, and even when the request is unacceptable. They just want to see their child happy, and to have nice thoughts towards them.*

*The worker that never says no to the boss; the one that we call 'the crawler'. They fear losing their job, and desperately need to be accepted and wanted.*

We can be aware of any of these behaviours in others, my friends, but we are not always aware of these behaviours in ourselves.

## Our fear

When we find ourselves buying things we don't want to buy, going places we don't want to go, being in company we do not want to be in... it's because we are afraid to stand up and say, 'Sorry, I have something else that I would rather be doing.' We are afraid to be honest in case we feel guilt. And we expect to feel guilt, because we go over in our mind how we would feel if we were in the other person's shoes.

We have learned to feel guilt throughout our lives, because we have been told by our role models that when we have done something that does not suit them, we should be ashamed of ourselves. So, our automatic reaction when we are not pleasing others is to feel guilt. And we expect other people to have the same thoughts, feelings, and behaviours as ourselves, so we expect them to feel how we would feel. Wrong! There would be no need for communication if we all knew what each other was thinking, would there? But what we have to understand is that we do not need the praise of other people to feel good about ourselves, or to feel happy, or to be who we want to be. Just because other people have responded to us in a way that makes us feel uncomfortable, doesn't mean that we have to feel guilty.

Our happiness does not lie in another person. We hold the key to our own happiness; no-one else can make us happy and no-one else is responsible for *our* feelings. And if we stay trapped in this horrible fear, we also die inside.

## Why do we behave this way?

We seek approval and fear conflict from other people because that is what we have learned within the environment that we have grown up in. We simply do not know any other way. It's a straightforward scenario:

*We have learned that for us to be happy, we must be pleasing the other person; when we are not pleasing the other person, we are afraid there will be conflict.*

*When there is conflict, there is a struggle for control; when there is a struggle for control, someone has to be wrong.*

*We do not want to be the one that is wrong, because if we are wrong we will then feel ashamed of ourselves, and no-one likes to feel shame.*

*So, we would rather do as the other person wishes rather than feel guilt or shame. Self-seeking behaviour leads to either us trying to control someone, or the other person trying to control us.*

Either way, my friends, this has to be addressed for us to love ourselves unconditionally. And now that you are aware of and understand why we all seek approval and have a need to be liked, loved, and wanted, surely you want to change it?

As we all know by now, change is very difficult, especially when we don't understand properly. This book is about understanding, awareness, and learning how to love. Its goal is to take you from a place of darkness into a place of light, where you truly belong. It's to help you to identify and change those horrible feelings and emotions and to lead you through the process of change.

But before we can change, we have to be willing and honest, and tired of hurting. So, I'm hoping this next section will help, because we have to learn to please ourselves and be comfortable with ourselves if we want to be truly happy and proud of ourselves.

## People-pleasing

Why do we people-please?

No-one likes to feel as if they are left out, as if they are on the outside looking in; feeling excluded makes us feel lonely. So, unconsciously – consciously for some of us – we please other people. And this all stems from the peer pressure we felt as children and teenagers but never recognised.

## Our belief

We have a belief that being nice to other people is doing whatever they want us to do for them, even if it's something we don't want to do. Sometimes we find ourselves in a position where we volunteer ourselves without thinking – only to think later, 'What am I doing this for?' By that stage, we are angry inside but afraid to say anything in case we make a bigger fool of ourselves. It's often the case that we agree to do things for other people before we even think about what it is we are agreeing to. How insane is that?!

## Feeling sorry for others

Empathy is to understand; sympathy is to feel sorry. When we feel sorry for people, they begin to tell us their problems. Often, we then offer to help them, but that can lead us to finding ourselves with responsibilities that are not ours. Without thinking, we befriend people and tell them, 'Just phone any time, or just pop in.' But we don't realise that can lead to us being overwhelmed by other people and their problems. They start to take over our lives and, although we resent it, we are afraid to be honest with them. After a period of time, we start to see that what we are doing is wrong, and we know deep down that the only way for it to stop is for us to put boundaries in and learn to say: No.

But we worry about how we are going to feel when we have to say NO, and how the other person is going to react. We think about them rather than ourselves. 'What they are going to say? How they are going to feel? What they will think of me? Will they talk about me? Will they give away any of my secrets that I've told them?'

We are afraid of other people talking about us, because we have all done it ourselves at some time in our lives. We've all given our opinion about someone or something that was none of our business.

## Volunteering

Volunteering ourselves – before thinking about what it is we are really getting ourselves into – makes us feel important; someone else wants us, and we get their undivided attention. Some of us even go a step further and find ourselves committing another person's time by volunteering their services without even asking them! That really is people-pleasing in the extreme.

There are times, though, when people-pleasing can end up causing us worry and discomfort. If we tell someone that we will get them what they need, then we start worrying about whether we can actually deliver our promise and what will be said if we can't.

## Getting hooked

Often people drop hints and we just jump in without thinking. 'What was that you were saying? Oh, I can do that for you; I've got one of them if you want it; I am going there, do you want a lift? Do you want me to give you a hand?' We hear what people are asking in their roundabout way, and before we stop to think… it's done, we have agreed to something, and we are not even sure if we wanted to. But now that we have offered or agreed, there is no going back. After all, what would they think of us if we say we're not doing it after saying we would? The resentment and annoyance builds inside of us, and by the time that we have to do whatever it is, we don't enjoy doing it because we are so angry at ourselves for being weak.

## The family

The people that we please the most are usually the people that we love – our parents, grandparents, partner, siblings, children, and close friends. Some of us we will go to any lengths to please the people that we care about most in the world. These are the people that we want to feel loved by and the ones that we want to be happy.

If we're being honest, though, we tend to feel the pressure more from our family than we do from anyone else. They are the people who put conditions on us and call it love. And since we are being honest, my friends, most of us don't act the same way in front of our parents and grandparents as we do with our partners, friends, and children.

## Our parents

Our parents are the people who we strive to please the most; we spend many hours worrying about what they think about us. Some of us will go through life *always* seeking approval from our parents.

There will no doubt have been times as children when you have been compared to your siblings, if you have any. Perhaps you were told, 'I don't know why you can't be more like your brother/sister/cousin?' This makes us feel inadequate, because we want to be shown love from our parents. And the less we feel loved by them, the more we will strive to please them. For our ego tells us: if our parents do not love us, then who will?

They don't realise that when they criticise us, we are left always trying to win their admiration. For example, when we have done something that we know they won't like, we spend time worrying about how they will react to us. 'What they are going to say? What they are going to think? Will they still love us?'

Those same parents are the people who have demanded that we have the same thoughts, feelings, and behaviours as they have. Then they disapprove of our behaviour and the way that we think, because they can't see themselves in us. Isn't life a little crazy?

## Our partner

If we love someone, we believe we will do anything for them. If they are happy, we are happy. This is co-dependency, and when we think and behave in this way, we can find ourselves doing whatever it is that they want us to do. They might even take on the same role as our parents. They might tell us how to dress, who we can be friends with, where we can and cannot go, how we should speak, what we should and should not be doing. And for the sake of peace in the home, we find ourselves doing whatever it is that they are asking us to do.

But a relationship should be about equality, and unless we have equality there is no respect or understanding.

We might have a partner who thinks that we will take on the role of their mother – a mother who enabled and spoiled them. They want us to take responsibility for them like Mummy did, where they do not have to do anything for themselves, other than go to work. They don't need to do any cooking, cleaning, shopping, washing, gardening, decorating, or looking after the children. They don't even know how their standards of living are maintained, or the cost of maintaining them. They still behave like a child, but with all the rewards that come with adulthood. Should we complain? Well, if we do, there is going to be conflict. So, for the sake of peace, we just continue doing what we are doing, we forget about our own needs, and concentrate completely on the needs of our partner.

## Our children

Children know how to wrap us around their fingers. They have learned at a young age how to get our attention and how to get what they want from us. As babies and toddlers, they learned that crying would get our attention; if that didn't work, they could throw a temper tantrum. Often, we gave in for the sake of peace, or because we were embarrassed by their behaviour.

When we have refused our children what we consider to be an unacceptable request (because that is what the tantrum started with), they will no doubt tell us that everyone else is doing it or everyone else has got one, then they begin to cry and use their emotional blackmailing. When this happens, we usually feel guilty and come to a compromise, thinking of something else that they could do or something else that they can have so that they will still be pleased with us.

But when we strive to make others happy at the expense of our own happiness, we will *never* be happy. We are doing whatever it is that other people want us to do, and not what we want to do. What's worse, when we please others while knowing that we wanted to do something else, we will dislike ourselves later on. Why? Because we are annoyed that we did not have the courage to voice our honest opinion; we did not walk away from a situation that we did not want to be in, and we never stayed true to ourselves.

If you understood that, you wouldn't suffer.

## Let's recap:

Bowing to pressure from others, seeking their approval, and pleasing them due to your fear of them, will prevent you from living the life you have been given. Now that you are aware of this, hopefully you will read this chapter again and again until the penny drops that these learned behaviours are the cause of your unhappiness, pain, and suffering.

Unless we become aware of our own suffering, then how can we change it?

Hopefully, your mind and heart are still open, as we are now going to look at the disappointment and hurt we feel through having expectations, and also the regret, shame, guilt, and anger we feel through not knowing or understanding.

# Chapter Four

## I didn't know I was doing wrong

### I wish I hadn't!

We have all said and done things in our lives that we shouldn't have done, things that we later regretted and felt guilty and ashamed about. And when we think about these times, we feel bad about ourselves. The thought lowers our mood, and we ask ourselves, 'Why did I do that? What was I thinking about?' We end up hating ourselves and wishing we could turn back the clock.

But that kind of regret is pointless. The things we have said and done, which we shouldn't have said and done, have happened. They are in the past. We weren't thinking about what we were saying or doing at that moment; we simply lost control of ourselves because we weren't getting what we wanted. Feeling bad about ourselves is our spirit's way of letting us know that we have done something which goes against the laws of spirit, and as we know by now, these laws are based on love and compassion.

If we think about it, most of the things we feel bad about were not planned. Most of our negative behaviour is a reaction to something we heard or saw that we were not expecting to see or hear. We didn't start the conversation thinking, 'I am going to say this… or do that.' We were just having a conversation and we didn't like what we were hearing. We either didn't like the tone with which we were being spoken to, or the words that were telling us we were not going to get whatever it was we wanted.

When we hear or see something that we feel uncomfortable or unhappy with, it triggers a feeling which causes a chain reaction. It's a pattern of behaviour that we have used since we were children and learned on an unconscious level from our parents. The feeling that is triggered is fear! Our fear is triggered because what we are hearing or seeing is not what we want to hear or see, but before we know it, our fear has turned to anger. When our fear becomes anger, we stop thinking about what we are saying or doing, and our tongue takes on a mind of its own.

The people we display negative behaviour around are the ones that we say we love the most. They are the people we know how to play; we know what to say to them, and which words and behaviours will get us what we want. We use patterns of behaviour with them that we have used since we were children, because these behaviours worked for us when we were younger. The problem is that when we were children, we didn't have a conscience; we behaved badly but then forgot all about it. Now that we are adults, we feel guilty and ashamed and it plays on our conscience. We learn to feel bad about ourselves, yet we still keep doing the same things over and over again. Why? Because we don't know how to stop it. We don't know how to change it. No-one has ever explained to us that we can stop and think about what we are doing and that we do have choices.

The hardest person to forgive is yourself, my friends. We can forgive other people for what they have done or said. Sometimes it takes a while, but we can find it in our hearts to forgive. Yet that's not the case with forgiving ourselves. This is because we were never taught to learn from our mistakes. We were taught to feel ashamed and guilty.

No-one explained to us that there would be times in our lives when we wouldn't like what we were hearing and seeing, and as a result we could be in danger of reacting in anger and then feeling bad about ourselves. It was never explained to us that our tongue could take on a mind of its own, and we'd end up saying things that we didn't mean and behaving badly without even thinking about what we were doing.

We were never taught about self-discipline or how to keep our minds focused on what we are saying or doing. Nor were we taught to look at the effect that this negativity could have on other people and the consequences to our own mental health. We used this behaviour as a child when we could not communicate and there were times when it worked for us, so we unconsciously continued to use it.

Think about this. Has anyone ever explained to you how to keep your focus on yourself, and how to recognise when you are in danger of losing control? Have you ever been asked to think about what triggers your emotions, or when your tone of voice and body are warning you that you're in danger of saying something you shouldn't or behaving badly?

If you have never been taught self-discipline, then how can you learn self-discipline! If you think about it, everything that you know today someone taught you. They showed you what to do, and you copied them and practised until you could do what you had been shown.

We were never taught about self-discipline, though, because our teachers – usually our parents – never learned it either. Instead, we have all been taught that when we have said or done something that we shouldn't have, we should feel shame and guilt. And that is exactly what we do! We think about something that we shouldn't have said or done, and automatically we feel shame and guilt. And we find it near impossible to forgive ourselves.

We are harsh judges of our own behaviour, giving ourselves a really hard time for the smallest of things. And because we haven't learned how to forgive ourselves, we just continue making the same mistakes and giving ourselves more and more things to feel ashamed and guilty for.

Look around you. If there are people you have hurt in the past but who are still in your life in the present day, they have obviously forgiven you or they wouldn't be around. Yet we don't think about that, do we? All we think about is how ashamed we are of how we hurt them. And once we start to think about one thing, we then begin to think about other incidents, and the more we think about them, the guiltier we feel.

Don't worry. Soon you will use your guilt to grow. For if we didn't feel guilt, my friends, then how would we know what to change?

Things that we have done in the past that we shouldn't have done will resurface until we deal with them in a spiritual manner. When these things resurface, they do so because the only way we can cleanse our soul is through honesty and taking responsibility for our negative selfish behaviours. Doing this leaves us feeling good about ourselves, because these are the things that have suppressed our spirit and which keep us depressed. They have been buried in our unconscious mind for a long time... but it takes time for us to forgive ourselves!

Undoubtedly, we *will* keep thinking about them, but each time we think about what we shouldn't have said or done, the depth of the feeling and the length of time we think about it will become less and less. This is called 'the letting go process'. Each time we revisit things we are ashamed of, these emotions become less harmful to our spirit. We can be grateful that we now know that they were wrong, and begin to measure our own progress.

Then we can begin to think, 'The past is gone, and there is nothing we can do to change it. I have learned from it, and I am grateful that I will not be doing it again in the future.'

It is the future that counts now, my friends; the past is something for us to learn from. And as we go through the process of self-forgiveness, we will find that every time we think about what we shouldn't have said or done, those feelings of shame and guilt will lessen.

When we start to feel that guilt and shame, we can challenge ourselves by thinking, 'If I didn't recognise that, and feel like this, then I wouldn't be able to change it.' We can think about the things we did which we no longer do... and then find something to occupy ourselves. This will help to lessen the feeling, because our minds become focused on something else. Take action, be grateful, walk, clean, go for a bath, talk to someone, take up a hobby, put on a cd. Make a list of things to do when you feel guilty, and the more you practise doing these other things, the less time you will spend feeling guilty. Out with the old, in with the new.

We have to realise that it is actually a good thing when we remember all those negative thoughts and behaviours, because they are at the root of our depressed feelings. All the money in the world and all the things we have won't change how we feel inside. The only way we are going to feel good inside, my friends, is by stopping the things we do that make us feel bad.

What we are doing is clearing the wreckage of our past, learning from it, and growing at the same time. The thing about life is we can only learn from experience; there is no other way to learn, so please try and be grateful for what your experiences can teach you.

As we've explained already, most of the things we do were learned from other people on an unconscious level. And no doubt you've been adamant at some point that you wouldn't say certain things or behave in a certain way... but out of habit, you did – and still do.

We have all sworn at some point in our lives that we wouldn't act or react in the same way as our mum or dad, yet when we reflect on the past we often find that we did turn into the very people we swore we wouldn't!! We just didn't know that as children we learned from the people we lived and socialised with, so our minds were programmed with the messages we heard and saw.

When we are in physical pain, we go to the doctor or we take some medicine; if we are in emotional pain, we might see a counsellor, therapist or psychologist. But we all know that we can see the doctor regularly and take medicine for a long time, or go for session after session of therapy, and still feel as if we are getting nowhere.

The people who do get well again will tell you they had to change their behaviour, their thinking, and their attitude, before they found peace again. This book is all about helping you to finally understand and become aware of your pain, and hopefully one day soon you won't need any therapy or medicine as you will be strong enough to heal yourself through awareness, understanding, and a willingness to be free from pain.

Each chapter is designed to give you the awareness and understanding you need, and by the end of the book, hopefully you will have found the courage to change. And courage is what you will need for the next few pages!

Having expectations can be extremely painful, especially when we aren't even aware that we have any, or that we have a habit of putting them onto others.

## Expectations

What are expectations? Expectations are how we picture, imagine, dream or plan how things will be in life. In this picture which we create in our minds, we decide how we want others in our life to fit in – the way they behave, the way they think, the way they feel. We want them to fit the image that we have created for them. Unfortunately, these expectations are conditions that we put on others and dare to call 'love'.

Expectations are also the cause of all the negative feelings that we have about ourselves and others. I would even go as far as saying that having false expectations is one of life's most painful experiences. When we expect, we feel worried, anxious, insecure, afraid, and hurt. When we have expectations of ourselves and others, we usually end up feeling anger. That anger is aimed at ourselves for what we should or should not have done, and at others for what they should or should not have done.

Why do we feel this anger? Because either we have failed to live up to our own expectations of ourselves, or others have failed to live up to our expectations of them. In other words, we did not get the result that we wanted, or things did not go the way we had planned. And when this happens, it can cause us to lose our sense of self-worth, our confidence can take a mighty dip, and we can become unhappy and disappointed as well as being angry.

## Expectations of ourselves

We all see ourselves as kind, loving, generous people who would not hurt or offend another person. We all have our OWN personal standards, morals, values, and ways of behaving. We set these standards because they make us feel good about ourselves, and these happen to be the rules that we live our lives by. But when we have failed to live up to our own standards – the ones that WE have set – we judge ourselves, we condemn ourselves, we feel anxious and insecure, and we worry. We begin to think, 'I wish I hadn't done that. I wish I hadn't said that. If only I had done this. If only I had done that.' We then feel guilty. And when we feel guilty, we are also ashamed of ourselves.

So, because we have failed to meet the expectations that we put on ourselves, we are now unhappy, disappointed, angry, and hurt.

## Expectation of others

We assume that others live by the same rules that we do. We expect them to have the same standards, morals, values, motives, and behaviours as us. When we interact with others, we expect them to give us the same response that we would give them. We expect others to treat us with the same consideration that we would give to them. For example, I am always on time when I meet my friends, so I expect them to be on time. When someone holds the door open for me, I always say thank you; when I hold the door open for others, I expect them to say thank you.

When they don't, I feel angry. I feel angry when others do not show me the same respect that I show to them. And when I do this, I then blame them for my anger – it is their fault that I am feeling the way that I do. But, really, it's not! These are my standards, my way of doing things; it is my expectation that others should treat me with the same respect and understanding that I show to them which has caused me to feel the way I do.

When others fail to meet my expectations, my thinking changes. 'How dare they treat me like this? How dare they do this to me?' But they haven't done anything to me, my friends. They didn't make me feel like this. Why? Because we are all responsible for our OWN feelings!

No-one else can make me feel anger or disappointment; it is my expectation that makes me feel the way I do. I didn't stop to consider that what I feel good with might not be what others feel good with. Therefore, it is wrong of me to assume that others think, feel, and behave the same way that I do.

## False expectations

We expect others to fulfill our image of them according to our thoughts and feelings and our understanding of how we think they will behave. But, being honest, we have already decided how they will behave by judging them. There are many ways in which we judge others – how they dress, how they speak, how they behave, who their family is, what area they live in, who their friends are, etc, etc.

When you meet someone who is dressed in smart clothes and speaks politely, you might automatically assume that they think they're better than you. You expect them to patronise you or look down on you, to feel superior to you. When we think like this, we are becoming insecure, uncomfortable, or inferior to people who dress smartly and speak politely. And when we expect to feel inferior, believe me, we WILL feel inferior.

Take an example. Your son or daughter has a new friend who is a member of a well-known family. This family is not known for being nice so, again, we expect this child to live up to the family name. We fear that our own child will get up to no good because that family has a bad name. So when our child goes out, we begin to worry and think 'what if?'. Our expectation of what we think might happen leaves us feeling anxious and worried; we are afraid that our child will copy the behaviours of this other child. But we are gathering false evidence! We have absolutely no proof that the other child is going to be a negative influence on our son or daughter.

It's the same when we meet new people who later become our friends/boyfriend/girlfriend. At first, it seems that we have a lot in common; we share our problems and our dreams, which are similar. We assume because we seem to have things in common that our thoughts, feelings, and behaviours will be the same. Initially, we don't notice that they are different, because we have a shoulder to cry on, someone to go out with, or someone to share our time with. We no longer feel alone, we begin to feel as if we fit in, that we belong. And we assume that our new friend has the same thoughts, feelings, and behaviours as we do.

We believe that they will show us the same consideration that we would show to them. For instance, I wouldn't pop into my friend's when it is mealtime, so I don't expect them to pop into mine. I don't plan ahead and fill my week in, deciding what I am going to do and with whom; I don't expect my friends to, either. We seldom take the time to get to know others and find out who they really are or what their standards, thoughts, and feelings are. We just assume and expect that they think the same way as we do.

It's not until we feel uncomfortable with their behaviour and their ideas about life that we finally realise we are not compatible. When they don't live up to the expectations we have of them, we start to drop a few hints. We disguise what we are trying to say, because we are afraid of speaking the truth and of being honest. We then begin to feel uncomfortable, but we can't ask them to leave or tell them it's over. Why? Because we expect to feel guilty if we say what we really feel, and our expectations have put us into a situation that we now feel uncomfortable with.

Unless we change, my friends, we will always continue to live in fear; the fear of how others will react to us for being true to ourselves. We expect them to know how we are feeling without actually saying how we feel, so we cause our own anxiety, worry, and fears. Why? Because we expect.

## Expectations from others

As we expect from others, others also expect from us. They also have their own standards, morals, values, attitudes, and behaviours that make *them* feel good about themselves. They will no doubt expect us to live up to their standards and will blame us for their feelings.

When we have two people who are unaware of their expectations, it leads each to thinking, 'I have done nothing wrong! How am I to blame? It's your fault that I am feeling like this. If you hadn't said that, or done that, I wouldn't be feeling like this.' Both parties are being irresponsible, both have reverted to blame, and both will hurt.

## Taking responsibility

When we have expectations of others, we will always feel fear – fear that we have lost control. We feel fear because we are not getting what we want; we are not getting the response from others that we want. It's a response that we feel we need in order to fulfil our image, the image that will make us happy, the image that meets our needs. We are seeking our happiness from other people through their response and behaviours towards our own ideas of how they should behave.

These are the conditions that we put on others and call them 'love'. But that idea of love is one that does not allow others to be themselves. It's an idea that stops us from getting to know people and who they really are, or even loving them for who they are and not who we think they are or who we want them to be. Our expectations can only lead to self-seeking behaviours, control, manipulation of others, bowing to peer-pressure, and people-pleasing.

## Why do we have expectations?

Prejudices are not just about racism or bigotry. Expectations are prejudices – they are conditions that we put on others and call them 'love'. 'I will love you if and when you meet my standards.' We are not aware of these conditions because they are learned; they are learned from our parents who learned them from their parents.

Our parents learn to meet their own needs through us – children who will make them proud, who will behave, think, and feel in a way that suits them. Children who will achieve all the things that they never achieved; children who will not make the same mistakes they have made. But parents don't realise that it is not what we have or have not got that causes our unhappiness, it is the conditions that others put on us that causes the worry, anxiety, anger, and fear. Expectations are the conditions we put on others and others put on us, and call this 'love'.

Okay, let's pause for a minute. Taking what you have read so far alongside your own experience with life, you may sit back now, close your eyes, and say to yourself, 'Am I doing something wrong here?' Well, if you are thinking that way, that's great, because you're now questioning yourself and opening your mind. It's not always about having your way all the time or always having to be right and in control. It's about trying to be honest with yourself without punishing yourself. It's about saying to yourself, 'Maybe my way or my will isn't working out any more. I think I've had enough pain, and I'm being truly honest with myself. I couldn't have done it any other way, as I didn't know there was any another way, but now that I understand there is, I can begin to change. I can finally begin to love myself.'

But for us to get to that point, we first have to understand ourselves, what happened to us, and why we hurt so much. In doing this, we break the cycle of dysfunction within our lives and the lives of our children, and we become powerful examples to others around us and within our own communities.

So, let's take a look at our picture of happiness in more detail, and hopefully this may open your mind even further.

## Our picture and search for happiness

We gave a short example earlier of where this picture of happiness begins – the one we painted as children, either at home, nursery, or school. Now, this just isn't any picture. This is a picture that every child draws on paper, unconsciously and unaware that it becomes planted within our minds. The perfect family picture with the lovely big house, car in the driveway, sunshine or a rainbow. and the two-point-four children holding hands with Mummy and Daddy... and everyone is smiling. Then, as we grew up, our picture of happiness grew wings and we got caught up in the material world. We lost all our gratitude for the simple things we had as children.

We began to look at what others have that we don't have, and we picture in our minds that they are happy so if we had what they have, then we would also be happy.

These pictures we are creating of happiness are now in an album in our minds, and we keep adding to this album every time we are unhappy. We can chase and search our entire lives, not knowing or understanding that these pictures we are creating only bring happiness for a short time. But our minds tell us that if we have these things we will be happy all the time.

There's nothing wrong with having nice things, and of course at times they do make us happy and smile. That's fine. But it's not fine when we desire them, covet them, try to control and manipulate to get them, get into debt and steal and lie for them, and then believe and justify in our own minds that it's okay to behave and think like that. That's when, Houston, we have a problem! If we really believe that happiness comes from external things, material things, and other people, we will always stay trapped and we will continue to suffer.

We suffer because nobody taught us that happiness comes from within. And it's a choice we have each day when we wake up.

Sometimes, you might sit and dream about what you would do if you won the lottery. Even though you might later chuckle at such fanciful thoughts, deep down you really believe if you had all that money you would be happy. Happy in the sense that you could buy that big house you wanted, and that fancy car, the kids could go to a fee-paying school, and you could give up your job and go on shopping sprees and far-flung holidays. You could also clear all your debts, and maybe help your family and friends out.

Oh, if only! Don't worry, you're not alone here. Most people paint this picture and believe that if they had these things they would feel better. What we tend to forget about are the famous celebrities with lots of money who have died through chasing this picture of happiness. And the ones who ended up in Rehab for drug and alcohol misuse and severe mental health problems. We tend to forget that these people also had thoughts like ours, but when their dream and picture became a reality, it also became their worst nightmare.

What we think and believe will make us happy is coming from our minds, and not our hearts. We have learned from our homes and environments, the media and press, that being happy is being rich. Rich in materialism, nice houses and cars, maybe even a private jet for those who go over the top, plenty of money, attractive husband/wife and several beautiful children, nice jewellery, all the boys' toys and gadgets, and the best of holidays. Basically, we don't have to work in this picture we're creating and dreaming up, and we really do believe these material things will bring us joy, happiness, and peace. We see people in advertisements having fun on holiday in a beautiful country, gorgeous beaches with stunning scenery, and we think... I wish. Or the log cabin, peaceful and serene, a place of beauty, and we think... I wish. Or the busy, exciting way celebrities, pop and film stars, footballers, etc, live their lives, and we think... I wish.

It's the same story in the housing schemes of Glasgow and in every area throughout the world where there is deprivation, neglect, and poverty. Young children within these schemes see older boys making money doing illegal things and being able to buy expensive jewellery and gadgets, wearing the best of clothes, driving their own cars. And when you don't have much and life is grim, it is understandable that temptation can get the better of you.

Sometimes what is pleasing to the eye, though, can land us in a load of trouble. That picture of what we believe will bring happiness forgets to include the stories in the media about these celebrities getting divorced, having affairs, being charged with assault, fraud, shoplifting, drug and alcohol abuse, committing murder, going to prison, etc.

It doesn't matter how much money and wealth you have, you are who you are and you can only be the person you believe you are. That's why not all famous people are the same; some stay clear of the limelight because of the way they have learned to behave and conduct themselves, whilst others love and crave the attention and can't get enough of it. And it's not just famous people this happens to. I would go as far as saying at least 90% of us humans chase this picture. Why do you think the world is in such a mess? We are all aware of the greed and ignorance, poverty, wars, addictions, homelessness, suicides, inflated egos, and the massive mental health problems throughout the world. This is the 21st century, and it's worse than the centuries before. We live in one big cycle of dysfunction because these negative learned behaviours have been passed down from one generation to the next. And the only people who can break this cycle are those who become aware of it and recognise the damage that these behaviours have had on their own lives and the harm they have brought to others.

When we get to that point in our lives, when we finally surrender to our old ways of thinking and behaving and become willing to change, we will understand that we really did believe it was normal for us to be doing what we were doing.

When we begin to search and chase this picture we created that certain people, material things, and loads of money will make us happy, then we are heading for a disaster. We see it happening every day to people, but think it will never happen to us. Think of the millions of people throughout the world who are homeless, caught up in addiction, mental health problems, incarcerated, and on prescribed medication. What about those you knew earlier in your lives, those you hadn't seen in years, and maybe one day in town you see them begging, homeless, and addicted? No doubt they once thought that it would never happen to them.

This journey that we're on can be very painful, and if we don't understand what has happened to us, why we are here, and what our purpose in life is, then we will always stay trapped in darkness and in fear.

Every day there are lessons for us to change and for us to be grateful, but we don't see them. Instead, we just accept that it's normal within society for people to suffer. The planet is falling apart and so are the people that live in it.

Maybe if I give you a few examples it will help you to understand that it's nobody's fault, because we didn't know any better. We didn't know that the way we have learned to treat ourselves and others, and the way we think about ourselves and others, is why we chase and search for this picture of happiness in the first place. No-one ever taught us about happiness and how it's created. So, if we weren't taught, we can only go by the lies our mind is telling us. And since we're not aware of our conscience or ego yet, we just do what everyone else does: we look outside of ourselves, and we look at other people, places, and things to make us happy. We do this because it's normal; we do it because we don't know any better; we weren't aware of the things that made us unhappy.

## Happiness in others

As a child, you had no conscience, so you weren't aware of good and bad or right and wrong, nor were you aware that you were truly honest and had no fear. A child will look you in the eye and tell you to your face, 'I don't like you' or 'I love you'. It has no fear of how you will react, it doesn't analyse, it tells the truth, it lives for the moment. A child is comfortable within its own skin – it's innocent, vulnerable, happy, and content with what it has. But as we now know from the previous pages, we soon lose that innocence. And the things we learn whilst growing up, we take with us throughout our journey.

The journey of life is all about self-discovery, and part of our journey involves becoming aware of our insecurities. One of these insecurities is our dependency on others to make us happy. So, in simple layman's terms, I will try to give you an understanding of where we learned to become dependent and the pain which comes from not knowing or understanding what happened to us.

As a baby and young child, you depend and rely on someone to feed you, to change your nappy/diaper, dress you, take you to the toilet, clean up after you, play with you, and show you love. You also depend on them to be there for you, to pick you up and give you attention (if they're capable of doing so, that is). This goes on for a number of years whilst you are growing up, and unconsciously you learn to become dependent on others to care for your needs and wants.

As we get older, this dependency can become habitual and difficult to recognise and break. That is nobody's fault, my friends. If no-one is teaching us to be independent, to rely on ourselves, and to be responsible whilst growing up, then we will always rely and depend on others.

When we have children of our own, we're not aware of this because we are trying too hard to be good parents. But this dependency can be with us our entire lives, and with this learned behaviour there's usually a lot of pain. Remember, we're learning this but we don't actually know we are.

So, this is where it all started. This is where we learned to become dependent on others, and since nobody bothered telling us or teaching us about it, we have gone through our lives depending on others to be there for us, to do things for us, to love and give us attention. And when they don't or can't, we become insecure, depressed, hurt, disappointed, and angry.

Not being aware that we depend on others for our happiness and wellbeing can be tortuous on the soul. This learned behaviour eats away at all the goodness within us; it strips us of all confidence and self-worth, and we can't see it happening. We have never learned to love ourselves unconditionally. We haven't been taught that we alone are responsible for our own thoughts, behaviours, reactions, feelings, emotions, and happiness.

Just think: if we were taught as children how to deal with life and its problems in a loving, caring, spiritual manner, there would be no need to search for happiness through others or to be in so much pain.

Do you remember your first love? Or someone you were madly in love with, the one that broke your heart? Maybe you remember thinking and saying to yourself, 'This is it, this is the one for me. I love them with all my heart and soul, and I would walk on hot coals for them.' It's that picture again, my friends, along with the dependency that this person is going to make you happy. And as we all know by our own experiences, probably one of the most painful times of our lives is when we break up with our first love. Losing that person and knowing you can't get them back, coupled with not knowing how to deal with the feelings and emotions, and certainly having no awareness of the dependency you have on this person, can drive people insane – myself included. It can cause severe depression, attempted suicide (and suicide), drug and alcohol abuse, anger, resentment, rage and violence, stalking, and even murder.

We can't see the wood because of the trees. We can't see what we are doing to ourselves; we are unaware that we have put other people before us. We fail to understand why we are unhappy, and because of this and what we have learned since childhood, we believe happiness comes from other people.

Relationships can be very painful, but also very beautiful. But they are extremely difficult because of our learned behaviours and the picture that we have created within our own minds. We are conditioned by what we have learned and believe to be normal, but is your partner/spouse happy?

That's why every relationship we enter into, we just repeat the same pattern of behaviour. We either allow the other person to control us and treat us like dirt, or we keep saying, 'I'm sorry and I promise I won't do that again.' We can't see that our negative, controlling, selfish behaviours and fears are now a habit, and because we can't recognise them nor have the wisdom to change them, our relationships crumble and finally fall apart. If we really believe that it is normal to look for happiness in other people and fail to open our minds and learn from our own pain, then we will stay trapped in this darkness. We will always be searching and looking for love and attention from others, because we don't know how to love ourselves or how to create happiness within our own lives.

Our journey, my friends, is full of valuable lessons, and the most valuable lessons and our greatest teacher are our own experiences of pain and suffering. It's sad really, but hopefully this book will help you to understand why this happens and to use this understanding and awareness to change what you have always believed to be 'normal'.

Learning to love ourselves and being truly happy and comfortable within our own skins is just a thought away. In order for us to love ourselves and others unconditionally, though, we first have to understand what prevented us from loving. And to do this, we have to learn to be honest and have the willingness to go within and face our fears. You already have this courage within you; you've come this far.

Being codependent on other people for happiness is probably more common than you could ever imagine, so you're not alone here.

When I finally realised I was dependent on others, I was stunned at how insecure I really was... but that was just the start. For when I finally began to get honest with myself, it was then – and only then – that I was awakened to the people, places, and things I had latched onto throughout my life. And if you thought depending on other people is sad, then wait until you read about the other insecurities!

I'm no expert on codependency, but if you want to understand more about the subject, get hold of the book by Melody Beattie: *Codependent No More*. It's a brilliant read. I've only scratched the surface to raise your awareness and give you a little understanding. And as you have probably realised by now, I like to keep things simple.

At the beginning of this book, I mentioned that I once had no confidence or courage, was continually unhappy and angry, depressed and suicidal, but I had no understanding about life. Now I firmly believe that our own life experiences are our greatest teachers, and once we begin to get honest with ourselves and stop blaming, we can begin the process of change. That's why it might seem that I'm being a bit repetitive at times, but I do this for a reason.

I do it because change is difficult, and I try to explain things in a very simple way, without complication or jargon. I do it for those who, like me, lack confidence and courage, believe that they are worthless, and at times no longer want to live. I also do it for those who want to change but don't know how to. That's why I repeat certain things in the hope that I may save a life, that maybe the penny can drop, and finally we can stop blaming and hurting, and begin to forgive ourselves and others. And once we understand in simple layman's terms what happened to us whilst growing up, why we were searching and chasing this picture of happiness and looking for love in other people, places, and things, then we awaken to the truth. And the truth sets us free from the lies we have been telling ourselves.

There are so many distractions and temptations out there in the material world, my friends, and we can easily become attached to them because of our insecurities. We usually do this to help take away the sadness and pain we feel when things aren't going the way we hoped or expected them to (i.e, our picture isn't focusing), or maybe because something has happened in our lives or to someone else and we don't know how to process it, accept it, or deal with the thoughts, feelings, and emotions which have arisen from it. When something like this happens (remembering from the learned behaviours chapter), you will understand that we can only deal with these circumstances and issues the way we have *learned* to deal with them. And if our own mind has told us that we can't deal with them and we believe that lie, then that's when the trouble begins.

We have to be watchful and vigilant of the way we think and react to our own thoughts, because it's our own thinking which causes us to feel pain, hurt, anger, resentment, etc. Try this out, if you don't believe me. The next time you are hurting, look around you and you will find that you are alone – nobody is criticising you; you're good at doing it yourself, by yourself. And do you know the funny thing? If someone was to speak to you and treat you the way you treat yourself and speak to yourself, you would thump them. You would never allow it to happen. So, why do we do this to ourselves, especially when we don't want to?

### Let's recap:

There are three important lessons in this chapter:

+ If we live in a world of 'I wish I hadn't', then we will always feel regret, hurt, and pain.

✦ When we have expectations and we put these expectations on ourselves and others, we will always feel disappointment, anger, resentment, and pain.

✦ When we are chasing and searching for happiness outwith ourselves, again we will feel pain, loneliness, emptiness, sadness, and hurt.

There are lots of things we do to ourselves that are insane, and the next chapter will show how a simple reaction can cause absolute mayhem within our lives. We need to discuss how it's our own thinking that we are addicted to, and our own thinking which is causing all the pain. And we will take an in-depth look at fear, which is at the root of most of life's problems.

# Chapter Five

## See, hear, and speak no evil

### Reaction through sight and sound, and what we tell ourselves

The triggers to our negative and positive reactions are mostly through sight and sound. There are some of us, though, who will react to touch, smell, and taste, but most of us react to what we see, what we hear from others, and what we tell ourselves within our own heads. The most damaging of all is the sound of our own voice – self-talk, the ego, the chatterbox, the dark side, the voice of destruction. It has many names, but this is the one we really have to become aware of because this is the one which dictates our lives, controls us, and simply destroys us. Our own thinking and how we react to it has now become our biggest habit, our addiction. And if we are not aware of this, it will eat away at our souls and keep us trapped in that dark, lonely place called normal.

Let's look at some examples then, as this will help you to understand and become aware of these negative habits, and how we react to what we see, hear, and tell ourselves in the way we have learned to react throughout our lives.

For example, you're on the phone to your friend, and you're having a laugh and have arranged to meet up for a coffee and a catch-up. Now, remember, you were laughing. You put on your coat and, as you approach the door, you SEE this pile of letters lying behind the door, and one or two of them look important. Within a split second, your mind has begun to spin its yarn and tell you (without you even opening the letters!) that it's bad news of some sort. And within that split second, you have stopped laughing and smiling and started to react to whatever it is your mind is telling you.

Now, let's re-run that situation. Within that split second, because you SAW those letters which looked important, you began to gather false evidence and it changed your mood from one of laughter to one of fear. You were telling yourself, 'It's a big bill; I'm going to lose the house; It's from the school, what on earth have they done now?; I've failed my exams; I didn't get the job, etc, etc.' And when you finally do get around to opening the letter, it's a big cheque!! Can you see now what fear is, and how we react and gather false evidence with no proof whatsoever? Yet we think nothing of it because we believe this behaviour to be normal!

Another example. You are out on the town with your friends, having a good time, and totally out of the blue you SEE your wife/husband/partner kissing someone on the cheek. Again, within that split second, you react. That is understandable, but how you react can be the make or break of your relationship. It's very easy for some of us to take that kiss on the cheek to the next level –he/she is having an affair; they're sleeping together, etc. Again, what you just witnessed with your own eyes has set off the trigger and allowed fear to creep in. And again, the ego will gather false evidence which will appear real in your mind – if you allow it to, that is. And you will, because it's 'normal'.

Or, you've decided you're going to watch the TV, and again you're in a pretty good mood. You've decided what you're going to watch, and without recognising within yourself, you begin to criticise, judge, condemn, argue, and get angry with the people behind a television screen – who can't see you, or hear you! Now this could be anything on the television you react to, especially when you get caught up in it. What you just saw and heard changed your mood, ruined your viewing and your night, but if we are honest, it's normal.

Or you're walking along the road laughing and joking with your friends, and as you turn the corner, you SEE someone who intimidates you, someone you just don't like, and they don't like you. Again, within that split second, you have stopped smiling and laughing and have allowed fear to take control of you. The voice in your head and those negative thoughts come in so quickly, you feel the sickness within your stomach, those butterflies, that horrible feeling of fear. Then the ego fills your mind with expectations, expecting and gathering false evidence about what's going to happen, and within seconds, you find yourself overwhelmed with these horrible feelings and emotions. And the funny thing is, the person smiles and walks right past you!

Final example. You're in the car, and you're in a really good mood and listening to your favourite music. All of a sudden, the driver in front of you seems to be moving very slowly, when really it's you who is driving too fast. Now, you can't overtake on this road, and if you aren't very patient and tolerant or have an accepting nature, then the voice of temptation will come in and take over. It might say things like, 'Oh no! I'm going to be late!' So you begin to panic, which can cause an accident. Or it could be, 'Who do they think they are, controlling my speed?' Or it could be the foul mouth, where you begin to get angry and road rage creeps in. This is when you start to take the situation personally, and someone could get killed, badly injured, and even end up in prison for a very long time. But the funny thing here is that the driver in front was travelling at the correct speed limit for that road. It is you who reacted and got impatient; it is you in a hurry; you that got angry. Yet, remember, just moments before that, you were laughing, happy, and singing along to music.

Crazy, isn't it? And all because you reacted and listened to your ego, the voice of temptation, the liar.

Our ego is the dark side. The ego is when you identify with what you are thinking about and believe it to be true. And because no-one has ever taught you how to challenge it or become aware of it, it now controls you.

If you are driving along and hit a pothole on the road, within a split second you lose your peace and calm, begin to get angry and look for someone or something to blame, and then go off on a rant. For most people, that one pot-hole can ruin their whole day.

Acceptance is a great gift, my friends, but we have to want it. We have to be sick and tired of the way our lives are and the negative way we react, then start to get honest with ourselves, or we will always be unhappy, moaning, and groaning.

Another example. You are going for an interview for a new job, and some of you won't have slept well that previous night because of what you were telling yourself. Lying in bed with all these different scenarios running through your mind, causing fear and negativity, by the time you get up, the chatter in your head is getting worse. And when you finally reach the waiting room, your mind is racing at 100 mph, you're panicking and sweating a lot, telling yourself you aren't going to get the job, you aren't good enough, etc. Doing this to ourselves is a habit. It's normal to react like this; it's normal to feel fear and expect the worst all the time. Isn't it?

Then on the other hand, you might be the over-confident one, the cocky one who truly believes the job is theirs. And when you don't get the job, you start to blame and get angry, because you haven't yet understood your ego, your expectations, your arrogance and pride. All these negative behaviours go against our true self, and when we go against our true self of love and compassion, we hurt.

It's the same when things don't work out the way we expect them to, we get disappointed. But when we change our negative reactions to positive ones, we will sleep at night and keep our peace, because we have finally learned from our past mistakes and pain. Taking responsibility for our negative learned behaviours and negative reactions will bring that peace.

There are so many triggers in life, but what we SEE, HEAR, and TELL ourselves are the main ones. This is learned, it's habitual, and it's the way we have been conditioned to react. It's the same when we SEE, HEAR, or TELL ourselves positive things – that brings on a smile, it makes us happy, and at times joyful and grateful. It's the negative thinking, the negative learned behaviours, and negative reactions that cause those horrible feelings and emotions, and it's our job to recognise them and challenge them in order for us to be truly happy and peaceful within.

This is your time, my friends. If you're up for the challenge, that is! This is something you *can* do. Yes, it will be difficult – no-one said it was going to be a stroll in the park – but if you look back at your life, you will find you have always got by because you're a survivor, a warrior, someone who never gives up. And now that you are beginning to understand that it's not your fault or anyone else's fault, you can begin to heal.

Have you noticed the common denominator yet? That's correct. It is our thinking. We might react through sight, sound, and what we tell ourselves, but it's our thinking that does the damage. Our thoughts are energy, and when we are being positive, loving, and compassionate, we experience the power of true love and happiness within us, through making that choice to be positive. And I think we know by now that negative thoughts and negative reactions only bring us continuous pain and unhappiness.

So please, keep your mind open for this next section, because it's all about our thinking. I hope the identification and answers are there for you, my friends, as our thoughts are what we need to change in order for us to be at peace.

## Thinking: the king of all addictions

Throughout the world, drugs, alcohol, gambling, sex, over-eating, retail therapy, etc, are all classed as addictions. Personally, I disagree – and I will explain why. I see all of these things as pain-killers – a dependency and a way of running away from oneself. We depend on these things in the same way we depend on other people to love us and make us happy. We use these things, and people, to numb the emotional pain we are going through, and it can take years and years before we will admit to this and learn to be honest with ourselves. Again, fear has its part to play in all of this. The fear of admitting to ourselves that we have a major problem within our lives, which is caused by having no self-control or self-discipline over our own thoughts, reactions, behaviours, feelings, and emotions.

As I mentioned earlier, we can only play the hand we have been dealt. That's why change is difficult, and that's why we become dependent on other things to kill our emotional pain. Drugs and alcohol will comatose us and help us to deal with whatever emotional pain we are going through at the time. This pain can come from the loss of a loved one, something that happened in our childhood, a break-up, separation or divorce, unemployment, a disease or illness, the loss of a job, shame and guilt, regret, resentment, fear, abuse, violence, self-loathing, hatred, etc. And since we are not taught how to recognise these feelings, emotions, or the cause of our pain and how to deal with them, we struggle and we hurt and we want to blame. Because when we are thinking negatively, we feel negative; and when we are being positive, we feel good. As you think, so shall you be. Now that sounds pretty simple, doesn't it? But as we all know by now, changing and breaking these negative habits is difficult.

Gambling, sex, eating, retail therapy, work, extreme fitness, etc, are other things we use to escape reality and to fill the void in our lives. And as we know now, that void is love. For if we loved ourselves, we wouldn't be doing these things to ourselves, would we? There are so many things which society classes as addictive behaviour, but each one is really just a dependency. A dependency which causes us to lie to ourselves and others, and can cause tremendous fear, mental health, aggressive and violent behaviour, suicides, death, families torn apart, prison, etc, and all because we have no control over our own thoughts, feelings, and emotions. For instance, an addict depends on their daily fix to get by, even though they often won't admit it. But when they can't get it, they are overwhelmed with fear and will do just about anything – and I mean anything – to get what they believe they need to get them through that day. And all this time they are listening to their own thoughts.

Now, this isn't just drugs and alcohol we are talking about here; it's all the dependencies. Those who can't get to work or the gym because of an illness or a broken bone can become very anxious and begin to panic, because their routine has changed and they don't know what to do with themselves. It's the same with the gambler who can't get their daily fix of adrenaline; they will beg, steal and borrow, con, manipulate and lie, in order to get what they also believe they need. The sex addict and those who buy, buy, buy, will display these types of behaviours and go to any lengths to fulfill what they also believe they need to get by that day.

Most people depend on outside 'things' to make them happy on the inside, and when they can't get these things, they panic and are then controlled by fear. When we depend on people, places, and things to make us happy, and can't recognise this, we will always suffer.

The problem is that we haven't recognised that we depend on these things, and we truly believe we need them or need to be doing them in order for us to get by in life. But here's my point: the actions or things are not our addiction, my friends. Our one and only addiction is our thinking, and I'm hoping that what you have read so far will have pointed this out. If not, I will explain in further detail so you may understand that it's our own thoughts that we are addicted to.

This is where the honesty has to be present within us, because we have to admit that we have insecurities and that these insecurities are now creating major problems within our lives. They are causing us to run away from ourselves, and when we do that, all hell breaks loose.

We know from the previous chapters that what we have learned growing up is what we believe to be normal. And as you know by now, normal hurts. All of our pain comes from not knowing who we are or why we are here, and because we are not taught about our journey and the lessons we need to learn in order to experience our true selves, life, and its purpose, then we hurt. We hurt because we don't know what's happening to us; we can't process where all this emotional pain is coming from.

We find it impossible to quiet our mind from all the negativity. It's telling us we can't cope or deal with this situation, and when we think like this we begin to panic, become stressed out, angry, and appoint blame. When we deny our weaknesses and insecurities, we can stay trapped in our dependency for years – for some, a lifetime. But I'm hoping this next part will really open your mind to what addiction really is.

Before our eyes open in the morning, our ego is waiting for us. And believe me, the morning is your most important part of your day. It all begins with a thought, and it all depends on which way you want to start your day. That's a choice we all have. We all have a choice to prepare ourselves for our day.

What we tell ourselves as soon as we wake up, and what we are thinking about the whole day, is our addiction. We are addicted to the way we think, and if we are *thinking* negatively every day, then we will *feel* negative every day. Our ego, the voice of lies, is very good at hurting us, so we have to be aware of it and its power. If you start your day off by listening to this voice and it's telling you today's going to be a bad day, then it *will* be a bad day.

If you are telling yourself you need something to get by for the day, and you really believe the lie you just told yourself, then you are denying your true self. Our own thoughts are telling us what to do, and we haven't recognised that what we are telling ourselves is coming from our own minds. We listen to our negative thoughts and then we act on them, and this is a major defect of our true character, which is love and compassion.

For those who are caught up with a daily dependency, their thoughts are usually pre-occupied with that dependency and they will experience the same pattern of thoughts on a daily basis, i.e. 'I need this; I have to be doing this; I can't get by without it.' They can't see that they are totally controlled and addicted by their own thoughts.

I have worked for over 23 years with drug and alcohol misuse, mental health, and just about every crisis you can think of, and during this time I have become a good listener. I know this now, because I can see that I didn't listen before! And during this time, I have witnessed the power of addiction, which is our thinking. I have worked with people who have lost limbs due to their dependency on certain drugs, and most of these people were under the age of 35. All of those people were warned that if they continued to do what they were doing, they would either lose another limb or die. Now, you would think or expect that they would take the lesson – but not the person with the dependency.

They need and depend on it so much that they have no fear of losing another limb or dying; their biggest fear is living without their drug of choice. That's why there are so many deaths within society, and each year the count goes up and up. And it's the same with mental health; it's at its highest ever. Even the doctors and nurses are stressed out, and society's way of dealing with it is to give people time off work or put them on medication.

We have to go to the root of addiction and mental health, which is our fears. And our fears are created by our thinking. Addiction and mental health are the same thing and should be treated in this way, as it's the thinking which is the problem.

I have also worked at a cancer unit, and again I saw the power of addiction whilst talking with some patients. I used to take some of them – many in wheelchairs – outside to have a cigarette. I'd be pushing the chair, and they would bring along their medication in the form of a drip on wheels. I would listen to their stories whilst they had their cigarette, sitting on their wheelchair with their heads shaved, holding onto their drip with one hand and smoking happily away with the other.

One day, I asked a few of them if their consultants had advised them to give up smoking. 'Oh yes,' they replied, 'but I need my cigarette, son!' All of them said that. Now, not all of these patients were terminal. I suppose I could understand why the terminal patients might want to continue to smoke, but those who were going through treatment and had a chance of the cancer being removed? Well, that's when I witnessed the power of addiction. They had been told to stop smoking to have a chance of living, but the fear of giving up something they had depended on for so long was far too much for them.

If you were offered the chance to live out the remainder of your life with the rest of your limbs, to have a chance to be free from cancer, and maybe live a fruitful life, wouldn't you jump at that? You'd think most people would. But when you have depended on something or someone for a very long time, it is difficult to break that dependency. And please remember, my friends, some of us are strong and others are weak, and it's not for us to judge.

If you look at your own life at this moment: what would you like to give up doing that's been annoying you and hurting you for a period of time? Then ask yourself, 'Why haven't I?' And there's your answer in a nutshell! Breaking any dependency is difficult, because our own minds are telling us what to do and we believe its lies. And the consequences that arise from listening to these lies we tell ourselves is extremely painful at times. We are addicted to the way we think, that's why there's so much depression within the world, and that's why there are so many people dependent on prescribed medication.

We become depressed because of our thinking. We are stuck within a pattern of thinking which has caused us to look in a negative way at life, ourselves, and at others, or there might be something we find very difficult to accept. But if we look back to before we became depressed, we will find we had some happy, funny, and enjoyable times. Then one day this dark cloud came over us and, before we knew it, that cloud was living with us on a daily basis. Our thoughts then changed from happiness to sadness, and we had no defence against them.

I spoke previously about the insanity of the human mind, that we can talk ourselves into self- loathing, self-criticism, belittling and even hating ourselves. But to do these things to ourselves on a daily basis? Well, now you know the power of addiction.

The dictionary meaning of addiction is: addicted to something; a habit that has become impossible to break; unable to give it up. This is what it says in the *Chambers Dictionary* which I have at my side, but I totally disagree with that! I believe that once we understand and change how we think, then our lives, health, and circumstances change as well.

If we use our negative thinking as our addiction – as I am trying so hard to point out! – you will find that the dictionary meaning is true.

It says 'addicted to something'; I'm saying it's our thinking.

It also says 'a habit that has become impossible to break'; I told you about the addicts with missing limbs who continued to use drugs, and the cancer patients who continued to smoke.

It also says 'unable to give it up'; I say, being trapped in fear prevents us from giving up and breaking *any* habit, including comfort zones.

Our own thoughts are so powerful, my friends, that they can bring us to our knees or lift us up to the skies. But we have to be aware that if we are thinking the same negative thoughts every day, then sooner or later we will become addicted to them. To go to the gym every day, to abuse drugs and alcohol every day, to gamble, to shop until you drop, to feel the need to have sex and masturbate every day, to feel depressed daily, angry, critical, resentful, etc... All of these are down to us listening to our own thoughts and really believing that what we are telling ourselves is true.

From first thing in the morning to last thing at night, we are responsible for our thinking, actions, reactions, feelings, and emotions. That is something we cannot deny any more. We cannot go through the rest of our lives blaming other people, places, and things for our current circumstances or for any emotional pain we feel. I understand that most of us learned to do this. We learned to blame because we never knew any better, but you know now that blaming and lacking in understanding and awareness has caused you to hurt.

I acknowledge that it's going to be difficult to change your thoughts and break your addiction, but I know that if you really want to be free from pain, you will do it. Especially now that you have the awareness and understanding that what society calls addiction is really our own pain killers – that something or someone we depend on to help us to get through our days.

It's not rocket science, my friends; in fact, it's pretty simple. The only thing that will prevent you from changing is your thinking, especially when you tell yourself you can't change. But that same thinking comes into play when you decide you have had enough and that you are going to change and be happy again. This time, your own thoughts have courage, commitment, and positivity behind them, and that is what you need in order to be free from your biggest addiction, which is negative thinking.

We are all aware of the power of positive thinking and what it can attract to us – good health, good feelings and emotions, good relationships, happiness, peace, contentment, serenity, and love. All of these things come through a choice to be positive rather than negative, and the only thing that can prevent you from even trying to be positive is your thinking, your fear, and your ego.

There are so many deaths around drugs and alcohol, billions of people are suffering from mental health problems throughout the world, and people are taking their own lives. If we do not know how to deal with our negative feelings and emotions or the circumstances we are being faced with, then we will hide and look for someone or something to comfort us. In most cases, we haven't recognised the cause of our pain yet, because we have never been taught how to recognise it or how to deal with it.

Whatever we are struggling with and finding difficult to accept, it's our thinking that's keeping us trapped in the pain. The king of all addictions is the negative way we have learned to think about ourselves, our life, and other people, and the only way to break this addiction is through being positive, grateful, and willing. Nobody tells us to do the things we do, apart from our own thinking, and hopefully you will find that out for yourselves very soon.

Now the only thing that will prevent you from being positive is fear. Fear is our biggest enemy, and it will prevent you from getting to know your true self. So, let's look at fear for what it really is. And once we understand it, we can begin to master it.

## FEAR: The root cause of all of our problems

Again, keeping it very simple... fear is the complete opposite of love. And since our true purpose is to love unconditionally, we have to learn to become aware of the things that are preventing us from loving. We looked at our learned behaviours – the habits we have formed, and the negative way we can react at times. We also looked at the pain which comes from not knowing or understanding who we truly are, or what happened to us whilst growing up as children, along with the pain we receive from blaming other people.

When I say fear is the root cause, what I should really say is it's the *only* cause. It's with us on a daily basis, slowly but gradually eating away at our souls. And the only way to be rid of it is by using the awareness and understanding you have, along with love. All love conquers fear. Yet, as we already know from the previous pages, love is difficult. But hopefully, after this part of the book, you will truly understand why.

Earlier, we shared some scenarios about fear, but not nearly enough. So, here are a few more for you to identify with, which illustrate why fear is the root cause of all our problems. Remember the definition – F.E.A.R.: False Expectations Appearing Real. Fear is something we create ourselves within our minds. We begin to gather false evidence within our minds, which then appears to be real, but we have no proof whatsoever that anything bad is going to happen apart from the lies our own mind is telling us. Armed with this expectation and illusion that something bad is always going to happen, we start to worry – and all worry is based on fear.

When we find a lump on our bodies, straight away we begin to worry and think of the worst scenario... and we haven't even seen the doctor yet.

Some of us get headaches, and straight away believe we have a tumour; stiffness in our limbs, and we tell ourselves it's arthritis; pains in our chest, and we decide we are going to have a stroke or a heart attack.

One day our eyes aren't focusing properly. We tell ourselves we are going to lose our eyesight and go blind, when really all we needed to do was to go and see the optician for glasses!

As we get older, and our wrinkles and grey hair appear, we begin to worry about how we look. But when we worry about it, the wrinkles get worse and the grey turns white.

We also worry about our jobs. You might hear a rumour that your employer is laying people off or that your work is closing. Straight away, you begin to worry and panic to the extent that your mind tells you that you are going to lose your house, and the family is going to be out on the street.

We worry about our children when they are out playing; we worry about them as teenagers, and even as adults! We run scenarios over and over in our minds of what can happen to them when they are out on their own or even out with their friends.

We worry ourselves sick, and for some people that brings on anxiety and panic attacks, which can be very dangerous.

We worry about money, and not having enough of it.

We worry about our retirement.

We worry about our health.

We worry about being late.

We worry about what people think of us.

We worry about getting old, about dying.

We worry, and worry, and worry, and the cause of all this worry and everything we worry about… is fear.

Fear and worry eat away at our souls. And this ages us and strips us of all the goodness which lies within us. Mental health, addictions, suicides, are all rooted in fear, and unless we understand this and dig out the root, that fear will always remain within us.

I had Bell's Palsy seven times, on both sides of my face. Bell's Palsy is a type of facial paralysis which results in an inability to control the facial muscles on the affected side. I couldn't close my eye or speak properly. I had arthritis on both my hands and also spondylitis of the spine, plus I chronically burned the lining of my stomach. I was caught up in addiction and mental health for over 20 years of my life, and all because of fear and worry. Because when we go against our true self, which is love and compassion, we hurt. And as we all know by now, we can hurt really badly.

All my pain and all my problems arose from not knowing or understanding anything about myself or about life. My anger, my fear, and my need to be loved caused all my emotional, physical, and spiritual suffering. But we all have to suffer, my friends, before we will ask for help, find a little humility, and begin to change.

I wasn't aware that my own negative thinking and selfish behaviours were the cause of all the pain within my body. I wasn't aware that we are spirit as well as human, and when we live by the laws of spirit – love, compassion, gratefulness, kindness, and empathy – we feel the love and the power within us, and we remain healthy. But when we go against it and live our lives in fear, worry, anger, blame, resentment, etc, then we suffer and so do our bodies.

There is always a cause and an effect; there are always consequences in life, good and not so good. The things which happened to my body did so because of my negative thinking. I know this because I lived with it, and now I live without it. I only live without it now because I took responsibility for the thinking and behaviour which caused it to happen in the first place. And that's why I can write about it.

And I'm not the only one. There are thousands of great authors out there who have used their lived experience to help others, but not everyone believes in the healing power which lies within us. The way to experience the healing is to take responsibility for the negative thoughts and behaviours which are causing your suffering and pain. Once you do that, you will experience true love and healing. And, please believe me, once you experience it, you will never doubt it again.

Doctors can't heal you or take away your fears. They can only prescribe medication or refer you to another professional. Either way, you will be put on some form of medication which will help you to cope with the pain, whether it is physical or emotional. And for many people, it can mean staying on that medication for life. We aren't aware that our own thinking is the problem, and unless we go to the root of our problem, which is our own fears, then we will no doubt have to remain on the medication and cope with the pain.

It's the same when people go for healing – Reiki, acupuncture, etc. At the time, it's great and that's why we go back for more. But when we finally get round to sorting out our own minds and become more grateful and positive within our lives, then we are able to heal ourselves, because the healing power comes through the mind. It comes through knowing who you are, believing and trusting in yourself, and having a true desire to be free from fear.

Fear has many disguises, my friends, and it's very cunning. For example, when we are in a relationship and we see someone kissing, hugging or flirting with our partner, we think it's us being jealous when really it's fear. Jealousy is looking at what someone else has that you want. In a relationship, the fear is that someone is going to take something which you believe is rightfully yours, when really it's not. We have no control over any human being, and when we allow fear to enter our relationships, we then begin to try and control the person through our fears. And as we all know by now, no-one likes to be controlled.

Fear is there every day, if we allow it. It's there when we think we are going to be late, for instance. And this can cause us to feel impatient and intolerant, which in turn brings on anger, resentment, blame, and more pain.

When we live in fear, we are really living in darkness. There is no light, no hope, no happiness, and certainly no love. Fear attracts negativity, and when we are in constant negativity mode, we are heading for disaster. Impatience, intolerance, anger, resentment, being critical, being judgmental, gossiping, greed, lying, seeking approval, selfishness, self-centeredness, people-pleasing, self-love, etc, etc, are all fear-based and come with severe pain.

Remember, problems don't fall from the sky and land on our laps. Problems are created through our own minds and our own negative thinking; and when we are being negative, we hurt; and when we hurt, we can hurt others as well. But once we begin to understand and become aware of what fear is, what it has done to us, and what it can still do to us, we can then work towards changing it.

The crucial thing to realise is that the only real problem we have is our thinking. Once we change our thinking, we are free from all of life's problems. I like to compare it to treating weeds. In the past, we sprayed weedkiller around but the result was only temporary, so each year the same weeds came back time after time. But by treating the root, the weeds were eradicated for good.

It's the same with life's problems. If we continue to procrastinate, deny, lie, blame, and use excuses, then our problems and pain will always remain with us; they will always come back. So, we have to get to the root of the problem and eradicate it once and for all.

There are also two specific words which we have to try and be aware of. Two words dressed up in fear, and which prevent us from finding happiness. And these two words are: What if.

## What if...

When we think about the future, my friends, we can become anxious about what lies in front of us. We start to worry and begin to think, 'What if this happens...'; 'What if they say this...';'What if they do that...'; 'What if I fail...' When we think 'what if', we trigger our fear! Our fear starts as a thought, which we then feed by thinking about all the reasons why we are frightened, and the more 'what ifs' we think about, the more frightened we become. That first thought leads to another thought, and then another thought and so on, and these negative thoughts trigger the sensation we feel in our bodies. We then believe that this is the sensation we are going to feel in the future.

When we become afraid of something that is in the future, it's because we have left the present moment. And our anxiety is also a feeling caused by taking our thoughts from the present moment into the future, perhaps thinking about something that we need to do later, or somewhere we need to go, or something that might happen. And when we do this, we always focus on the negative. As human beings, it is in our nature to think about the worst possible scenario and make ourselves scared. Yet not only do we make ourselves scared, my friends, but we paralyse ourselves with fear. Some of us even reach a point where we are afraid to try something new or go to new places because we worry ourselves sick about something that might or might not happen.

Even though we have no evidence that what we imagine is going to happen, will happen.

Ask yourself: How many times have I been frightened to do something or go somewhere, then when I finally got round to doing it, all the things I had imagined would happen, never happened? Most of the things that we are scared of never happen; most of them only happen in our minds. It could be that some of the things that we are afraid of have happened to us or someone else in the past. Fair enough, this can make us more cautious than usual. But it doesn't mean that it will happen again in the future. It's our minds that put all these obstacles in front of us and prevent us from doing things.

We think, 'What if this happens? What if that happens?' And with each 'what if' comes another reason not to try whatever it was we were thinking of doing. So we find all sorts of reasons not to go somewhere we haven't been before, and start making excuses up within our minds: 'What if I'm late? What if I can't find it? What will I say?' We don't challenge ourselves about the fact that everything we can do today and all the places we have been to in the past were all new to us at one time.

The fear that stops us the most is worrying about how other people are going to behave towards us. 'Are they going to like us? What they are going to think about us? Are they going to be nice to us? Will they talk to us? What will we talk about?' By the time we've run through all that, we start to think about 'What will I wear? Will I look smart enough? Will that be appropriate for the occasion?' So we have all these thoughts going round and round in our heads, crippling us with fear, sometimes causing us to panic. And when that happens, we find it easier not to go.

Look at your past and think of all the times you went somewhere new or did something for the first time, i.e., school, high school, college, work, joined clubs, went to new venues, moved to a new area, etc. Naturally, everything was unfamiliar to start with, but before long the unfamiliar had become familiar. People were strangers the first time we met them, and yes, we might have felt uncomfortable with them at the beginning, but the more times we met them, the more comfortable we felt around them. And some of these strangers ended up becoming good friends.

We allow our minds to wander off into dark places where we feel pain and become afraid of everything. And the reason we worry is because we don't trust ourselves that we can deal with whatever happens in life. We look at all the things that have happened to us and the feelings we have experienced, and believe that we can't cope. But in fact, the evidence we have is that we *can* cope, because we are still here to tell the tale of all the things that happened to us in the past. It might not have seemed that we were coping at the time, but the fact remains that we *did* cope and we *will* cope in the future.

Everyone has fears. Some of our fears are rational, because what we are scared of is dangerous, and that is based on facts. Then there are the fears that are completely irrational; they are based on our imagination and how we think something is going to be. How many times in the past were you scared to do something or to go somewhere? But in most cases, what you thought was going to happen, never happened! Usually 95% of what we imagine is going to happen never happens. Look at the times you have been somewhere or done something that you were terrified of doing, then thought, 'That wasn't as half as bad as I thought it was going to be.'

Everything that we have done in life was new to us at one time; we were all babies, remember, and had no fear at all. There was nothing that we were scared of then, because we hadn't yet learned about the dangers of life. We would put our fingers in electric sockets, touch things that would burn us, climb on top of things without the fear of falling off and hurting ourselves. We would put things in our mouths and eat them without knowing what we were eating, and we would speak to anyone who would speak to us. We would also wander anywhere without thinking about where we were going or if we would get lost. Children never think, 'What if'.

But we *learned* to be scared, and we learned to be scared by watching and listening to other people and what *they* were scared off. We also learned to be scared because of things that happened to us in the past, or things that happened to other people we know. So, when we start to let our mind wander off into 'WHAT IF', we have to learn to challenge the thought and ask ourselves, 'What evidence do we have that what we are imagining will happen is going to happen?' We have to learn to keep our focus on what we are doing in the here and now, because this is where the peace is. But, again, this has to be practised in order for us to find the peace.

## Digging out the root

Ask yourself, 'What is it I am frightened of, and why?' For this is the first step in practising honesty, and this is how you will begin to recognise your fear and dig out the root. At times in our lives we have all been overwhelmed with fear, and although we dislike the thoughts and feelings entirely, we never learn from the pain. Problems are created, my friends. Fear, anxiety, and worry are also created, and the only way for us to solve these problems is to take responsibility for them. If you knew you had a choice to live without fear and you knew how to prevent it from ever happening again, I'm pretty sure you would grasp the opportunity with both hands, because no-one likes to feel or live with fear. So, this is your time. Your chance to be free from fear has arrived.

You might be thinking, 'There's no way anyone can live without fear.' And that's ok; most of the planet will think like that because they have lived with it for so much of their lives. But once you understand fear, become aware of it within your life and have the desire to be free from it, I promise that you will be free.

You were free from fear as a child, and now you know that you unconsciously learned to feel fear. So, ask yourself, 'Do I really and truly believe I can unlearn this filthy habit?' And if the answer is yes, then what you have read and what you have still to read will take you through the process of change. It's not fair to tell someone, 'Just change your thinking. Be more positive and don't be so negative.' If change was that simple, the death rate wouldn't be so high, and prisons, Rehab centres, hospitals, and mental health projects would no longer be full to the brim.

You have to *want* to change, my friends; it's as simple as that. Without the desire and willingness, you will stay trapped in fear.

The root of fear began when we lost our innocence. We weren't born in fear, we learned it. And if we want to be rid of it, we have to dig out the root. In the *Wizard of Oz*, the cowardly lion asked for one thing. Now, he could have asked for anything, but he chose to ask for courage. He knew that with courage he could do anything, and he also knew he would never be frightened again.

You don't have to ask for courage, my friends. It's already there. It always has been, but it is fear that has prevented you from tapping back into it. This book is designed to help you to be free from the fear which is causing all the pain and negativity within our lives. Use your pain as your motivator. Be rid of this illusion and expectation, and learn to trust yourself.

The root has been there and growing within you for a very long time, just the same as all the insecurities we have learned. That's why it takes courage, honesty, awareness, and understanding to dig the root up and be rid of it for good. Once you decide to be free from fear, you ignite the fire within you, your spirit will awaken, and the changes will begin. Through your awareness and understanding of fear and your desire to be free from it, the root will die because your thoughts and actions are based on love – and all love conquers fear.

Later on in the book, we will look at the process of change, where we will teach you how to change your thinking and how to recognise your fear, rather than telling you what you need to change. Remember, we have all been living with fear for years, and when we live with fear our spirits are dead and there is no motivation or inspiration within us. There is no love; some of us might never have experienced what true love really is or how it feels. But trust yourselves. You will be free again, that I promise.

When we water a plant, it grows because we are giving it food. But if we stop watering it, eventually it will die. Fear is the same. When we stop feeding the fear, eventually it will die. We will have exposed the root through our awareness and honesty, and our desire to be free from fear. The way to kill the root and dig it out for good is to stop feeding our spirits with false information.

Replacing our negative thoughts with positive thoughts allows the love to come flowing in and for the fear to be uprooted and discarded for good. We now know what fear has done to us, we are aware of the problems and suffering it brings, and we are also aware and understand that it's our own thoughts which create the fear. So, now we are aware and understand how to be rid of it for good. The process of change chapter will help you to further understand what it is we need to do in order to be rid of all fears and insecurities. So hang in there, life gets better when we begin to understand who we truly are and the power that we have within us.

At times, the Universe will throw us a curved ball to keep us on our toes, so we have to be ready for it. There will always be something happening in life; some good, some not so good. It's the not-so-goods that are there to teach us, to build us up, and to help us to find the love within.

## Let's recap:

If you think of the three wise monkeys and what they stand for – see, hear, and speak no evil –then that's how I would sum up this chapter. For if we are always seeing the bad in ourselves and others, we will always hurt. And if we are always thinking negatively towards ourselves and others, listening to gossip and stories from others and colluding with them, we will always hurt.

And the same goes with what comes out of our mouths. Speaking and thinking in a negative way towards ourselves and others, without thinking about the consequences, will always come back to us in pain.

Hopefully you are now aware why and how you react the way you do. Once we begin to understand why, then we can begin to practise non-reaction.

Our next chapter is all about awareness, understanding, and acceptance. When we finally accept that there will always be something and someone to challenge us in life, we will keep our peace. But first, we have to accept it.

# Chapter Six

## Increased awareness and understanding of oneself

### There will always be something!

If we want life to be different, then we have to do something differ-ent. And if we want to be happy, then we have to stop doing the things that make us unhappy. We all know by now that we don't want to be spending our lives going round and round in the same circle, repeating the same mistakes over and over again, always thinking about how different we would like our lives to be. But the truth of the matter is that the only way our lives are going to be different is if we do something to make them different. If we look back at our lives thus far, we will see that there was always something going on, some obstacles and challenges, someone always trying our patience. And that's the way it will continue; that's life.

Once we accept there is always going to be something and we welcome it, knowing it is there for a reason and that reason is to strengthen us, then we are truly wise.

When we accept that it's not life or other people who need to change, we can retain our power. For at the end of the day, the only thing we have any power or control over is ourselves and the way *we* think and respond to life and to other people. We have no power over anything or anyone else, whatever happens is going to happen and there is nothing we can do about it. That's why acceptance is a good tool to carry around with you.

If we look at our past, we will find that we had no control over what happened in life or the way other people behaved, spoke to us, or treated us. And when we tried to make other people do what we wanted them to do or to give us what we wanted, it only resulted in us saying or doing something we later felt guilty about.

We had no control over life or other people in the past and we won't have any control in the future; things are going to happen, and people are going to do what they are going to do. Looking at past experiences and what you have read so far, you will find the only thing we will have any control over in the future is how we respond to life and to other people. How we think and the feelings we experience will depend on how we react to whatever happens in our lives and to the way other people behave.

It will be *our* choice, my friends. We can choose to moan and groan, get angry or disappointed, behave badly and be unhappy, or we can begin to accept that people are going to do whatever they are going to do and that things are going to happen which we have no control over. When we accept this, we will be at peace and feel good about ourselves.

It is inevitable that some things happen in life which can cause us to feel unhappy and sad, like people dying. This is even harder when it's people we love, but eventually we get through the grieving process and learn to live with our loss. It will be the same with anything that happens to us – plans which go wrong, things breaking down, other people behaving badly, etc. We will learn to go through a process where we will adapt and learn to deal with whatever life throws at us.

When we reach that point where we want something different from life, we first have to identify the cause of our unhappiness, then recognise when we are actually doing these things, and then change how we respond to them.

When we experience this lightbulb moment and identify the things we need to change, we will then have a choice to either feel guilty or feel good. But we have to recognise when we are doing these things in order to change them, and be grateful for recognising that this is something we need to change!

When we identify what it is we want and need to change, unfortunately we will still find ourselves doing the same things for a while. That's because we have been doing these things for most of our lives that they have become 'normal' to us, like a chain reaction stored in our unconscious mind. We do them without stopping to think about what we are doing or why we are doing it.

So, it's important to accept that we will still fall into our old patterns of thinking and reacting before we get to the stage where we will be able to stop ourselves. We also have to be aware that stopping ourselves once doesn't mean we are cured!

We have to learn to make a conscious choice, then reprogramme our unconscious mind – and this will take time, as change comes with patience and practice. It takes time and practice to learn something new. Think about it: there is nothing we have learned that we were able to do perfectly the first time round.

Everything we learned took time: we looked, we listened, and copied until we perfected. If you go to college or university to study, you're there for between two and seven years; it's the same if you decide to learn a trade, it's between three and five years. So, learning to change something that we have been doing over a lifetime is going to take time and practice. But the more we practise, the more natural it becomes. And when we do fall into our old patterns – no matter how long we fall into them for – the fact that we can recognise and stop ourselves means we will have something to feel good about.

We have to think, 'I might not be doing what I would like to be doing, but at least I am not doing what I used to do.' We also have to learn to measure our progress and remind ourselves what progress we have made, otherwise we might be tempted to look at the negative side. Telling ourselves, 'I know not to do that', 'What did I do that for?' or 'What an idiot!' only makes us feel guilty and we dwell on our actions because we are trying not to do these things any more. Please don't listen to those lies.

Until we learn to reprogramme our unconscious mind, we will find we will react to the same situations, the same people, or the same behaviours in people, as we always have. Our priority as we do this is to learn to measure our progress. The fact that we admit we have done something we shouldn't have done is a good start, because we can't change without recognising what we need to change!

We can then measure the length of time we were in our old pattern of thinking – weeks, days, hours, minutes, seconds – and each time we fall into that old pattern, the length of time we will do it will get shorter and shorter. Until, eventually, we will be able to catch ourselves in the moment.

When we react to other people in a negative way, we will be able to measure how angry we are now compared to how angry we were the last time we were in their company.

We will measure our progress by first admitting we shouldn't have reacted in the old way, then by measuring how good/bad our words and behaviour were, how angry we got, and how long this anger lasted for.

The thing about life is we can only learn from experience. And even when we do something and we think, 'I shouldn't have done that', the positive is that at least you now know you shouldn't have done it. So, well done. Through practice, you will be able to identify what thought patterns and behaviours you have that affect your whole being. You will be totally aware of who you react to and why you react, when you are likely to lose control of your tongue, and when you are in danger of behaving negatively.

Through practice and time, you will be able to identify who it is and what it is that triggers these thoughts and behaviours that are the cause of your unhappiness. This will allow you to think of different ways of catching yourself before you go too far.

Remember, my friends, the people we are most likely to behave negatively towards and say things we shouldn't say to, are our family and friends, or people in authority who are not giving us what we want. We are more likely to react to family and friends, because these are the people who we have known for a long time. We know when they are going to say no to us, and we know we can often wear them down to get what we want. They are also the people we feel the most guilt over when we have behaved negatively, because we love them.

However, on the plus side, we can usually read them like a book and anticipate how they are going to react and what they are going to say. So, instead of manipulation, we can use this information in a positive way to help us to keep control over our words and actions.

When their words, tone, and body language trigger a negative reaction within us, we will feel it in our bodies; this feeling is our fear, and within a split second it can change to anger. As we only have seconds in which to catch ourselves, we are not going to be able to recompose that quickly, especially when we are just learning to be mindful of what we are saying and how we used to react.

That means you need to have a plan of action ready. It could be to simply walk away, to mentally count to ten, to keep repeating to yourself 'Don't react. Keep your peace', or to just smile and give them no ammunition. Whichever way you prefer, remember, this is *your* journey and *your* life, and if your pride and ego hurts at first, it won't last as long as the feelings of guilt you have when you end up saying or doing something you later regret.

When our mood is changing when we are with other people, we will become aware of our thoughts and the sensations we are experiencing in our body. We will know when we have reacted and are thinking negatively, because our thoughts change and we start to think, 'I wouldn't do that', 'If that was me...', 'That's terrible', 'I couldn't do that', etc. And if there are other people there, we might want to ask them if they saw or heard what we did.

This is a warning to us that we are putting ourselves in a position where we will destroy our own peace of mind. We react to how other people do things because somewhere deep inside we are afraid that we are wrong.

So, what we have to do is decide: does it really matter any more who is right and who is wrong? What would we rather have – peace of mind, or something playing on our minds for who knows how long? And remember, it shouldn't really matter what other people are doing. We know from our own personal experience that when we have done something wrong it plays on our minds, so whoever it is that we are looking at will have to go through the same process as we do.

We get away with nothing in life; there will always be something. What goes around comes around, and it comes around for us to grow, to learn, and to be happy.

This book is designed to help us to seek out the behaviours which cause our pain and unhappiness, and these next few pages will surely do that. We all want to be loved, but can't recognise the things that are preventing us from feeling it and receiving it.

## We are all the same

We live in a world where we have learned to value people in the same way as those we lived and socialised with valued people. We have learned to judge and put labels on people according to their appearance, their accent, and what we think they are telling us. We have not learned to give unconditional love; instead, we have learned that there are conditions which other people should meet before they can be considered worthy of being treated as though they are one of our friends or family.

None of us likes to think that we don't treat others as we wish to be treated ourselves. We like to believe that we would do anything for anyone, and yet there are people who we wouldn't smile at or say hello to. This is a fact. We have learned to label people according to their appearance or what their accent is telling us about them; we have learned who we should be nice to and also those we don't have to be nice to. Some of us have also learned that there are certain people who we can be abusive towards, even though they have never done anything wrong to us. We do this without knowing we are doing it, but pay the price later.

We have not been taught that everyone has feelings, nor have we been asked to think about how we feel when someone has not been warm and friendly towards us. Usually the first people we learn to label are our neighbours, and then the people from the area where we live. Then we move onto other areas and, because we live in a multi-cultural society, that involves people from all over the world. There are conditions that are obvious: race; weight; religion; age; sexual orientation; which football team people support; the area they live in; how wealthy they are; the job they do, etc. Then there are people we are hostile towards because they have done something to someone we know or because we have heard someone talking about them. But we never stop to think that there are people who do things differently from the way we would, and who have different ideas about life from the ones that we have.

As I said already, we all like to think that we would help anyone who needed it and that we treat others as we wish to be treated ourselves. We don't think about the fact that we behave differently towards some types of people depending on how we have learned to label them. We have witnessed with our own eyes and heard other people do this, so we believe it is alright to behave that way. As children, we watched and listened to everything that was going on; that is what children do, they are curious. When people were talking, we noticed the tone of their voice and the words they were using, and whether or not they were being warm and friendly. We were aware of their facial expressions, if they were smiling or scowling, we could even feel the different vibes when they were talking to different people or about different people.

On an unconscious level, we learned to treat other people in the same way as our friends and family did, or do. Some of us not only learned this, but were told we must do this and we were too scared not to.

We have all either said or heard other people saying, 'I don't like foreigners.' When we do this, we are not generating love. We are generating hate, which leads to us becoming angry with other people with no valid reason other than what other people have taught us. Yet as a child, we would smile at *anyone* who smiled at us.

We have not been taught to respect people for who they are, that everyone has a right to live their life according to their own beliefs and values, and that others' different beliefs and values were learned from the people that *they* lived and socialised with. Empathise rather than criticize, my friends. Just because other people do things differently from the way we do doesn't mean our way is right and theirs is wrong; it just means that they have learned a different way from us. If we had been taught to give love unconditionally, we would have learned that we are all human beings with the same needs and we are all entitled to be treated with respect.

We all have our own idea of how things should be done and what we believe is the right way to treat other people. Do you think you really treat others as you wish to be treated yourself? Do you treat everyone you meet in the same warm and friendly manner you treat your friends and family? If not, have you ever asked yourself why? Have you ever asked yourself, 'What has this person ever done to me?'

This is how we learn to be honest. By questioning our negative thoughts and behaviours. Since our behaviour is 'normal' to us and we have been using it all of our lives, we don't give it a second thought. We don't question ourselves or our reasons, we just fall into a pattern of behaviour that has become normal to us. For all we know, the people that we discriminate against could in fact be very nice people.

We even put conditions on our friends and family. We treat them with love when they are doing what we want them to do; when they are not, we are cold and hostile towards them. We fall into patterns of behaviour where we try to control and manipulate them, and if that doesn't work we use emotional blackmail. We plead, beg, bargain, and threaten them, sometimes even resorting to violence, then we feel guilty and blame *them*. The conditions that we put on others are not so obvious to us but can cause major problems to our mental health.

When we observe people not treating others the way we would treat them, or not doing something the way we would do it, we become uncomfortable with ourselves and start focussing on the other person and what they are doing that we wouldn't do. We use phrases like, 'If that was me, I wouldn't do that', or 'That's terrible. How would they like it?' We think about all the reasons why we wouldn't do what we have witnessed the other person doing, and this confirms to us that the way the other person is conducting themselves is wrong.

Sometimes it reaches the stage where we can't stop thinking about what we witnessed, and the more we think about it the angrier we become. We then feed this anger by thinking about all the reasons why we wouldn't do what they have done. We do this to confirm to ourselves that we are right and the other person is wrong. It keeps playing on our mind, so we then go and tell someone else about what we have witnessed, and how neither of us would do that to anyone. Whoever we are talking to will no doubt feel compelled to agree with us, especially if they are one of our friends or family. They won't want to disagree with us, as they live their life by the same standards as ourselves!

Once we have the confirmation we are looking for, we will stop thinking about the incident for a while, but the thoughts will keep coming back. The truth is that we keep thinking about what we witnessed because, when we judged the other person according to *our* standards and values, we broke the laws of spirit. What goes around comes around; our spirit becomes disturbed because we are having hostile thoughts towards someone else when we are supposed to be having loving thoughts.

Our spirit knows that if we admit to ourselves that we shouldn't be judging other people, we will be free of these negative thoughts, and peace of mind and contentment will be ours. It keeps reminding us of this, because it wants us to be free and happy through choosing to be responsible for our selfish behaviours. And when we are thinking about what other people do that they shouldn't be doing – according to our standards – the only person that hurts is ourselves. The other person is away getting on with their life, so the only person it really affects is us.

And our reaction is caused by the fear of being wrong. We don't like the idea that we might be wrong, because if we are wrong it would mean that we would have to deal with the feeling of shame and guilt. We don't see anything wrong with judging other people, because we hear other people talk about someone or something they have witnessed or heard about someone doing something that they wouldn't do. And when we listen to them judging other people, we agree with them and confirm that what they are saying is right. But at some point, we are going to feel bad about what we have said and wish we hadn't.

When we allow what other people have done to play on our minds, it affects our ability to function as a person. We can become depressed and unable to sleep, and then can't be bothered doing the things we need to do. Our negative thoughts cause us to feel tension, aches and pains, and often headaches. We can even end up being

so judgmental and negative that we become isolated from life alto-
gether, and all because we have never been taught that what other
people do is *their* business; if they have made a mistake, it is between
them and *their* conscience; and if they do something different from
the way we do it, that doesn't make *us* right and *them* wrong.

We are all the same, my friends; we are all equal. It's only when
we are being negative and selfish that we hurt, and that's why it's so
important for us to understand *why* we hurt so badly at times. But
with awareness and understanding, a little courage and humility,
that pain and hurt will eventually leave us, because we will be living
by the laws of the spirit, which is basically love and compassion.

This next section is very similar with regard to people. You will
find throughout the book, and throughout your own lives, that most
– if not all – of our pain comes through not knowing how to love
ourselves and other people. And here's why.

## People shouldn't, but they do

The most common issue amongst us humans, and the one that
always plays on our minds and strips us of all our goodness, is the
way other people have treated us. Perhaps it was the way they spoke
to us, their tone, the words they used at the time, or what they did to
us. But we are unaware that there is a code of conduct within society,
and there is also the family and friend code of conduct, then there is
our own code of conduct. A code of conduct is each individual's idea
of how people should behave and how they should treat us.

We all have our own idea of love, as we discussed earlier; an idea
is something we create with our mind, a picture in our head. It is
our own idea when we say or think, 'If that was me, that's not what
I would do', or 'I wouldn't do that to anyone', or 'If they loved me,
they wouldn't say or do that.' These thoughts are our ideas.

And we have our own idea of how our family and friends should
show us love. We expect them to live up to their role according to
how we would live up to that role if we were them. We want our

parents, friends, family, workmates, partners, and children to treat us the way we would treat them, and to do for us what we would do for them. We want them to show us the same love and respect we would show them.

And when they don't? We feel angry or disappointed with them, then think about everything they should and shouldn't be doing for us. We see them as being selfish, and think about how their behaviour has now affected us, so then we blame them for the way we feel. The voice in our head says, 'It is their fault.', 'If only they had listened.', 'If they had done it my way.', 'If they hadn't done what they did, I wouldn't be feeling like this.'

We believe it is *their* fault because we compare what they have said or done to us with our own idea of what they should be doing. But we don't realise that our idea is created by our imagination, the part of us that creates pictures in our head. Yet what happens in our head is not real. Yes, there are things that on a moral level people shouldn't do, but in reality they do! And just because people shouldn't, doesn't mean they won't. It is our own expectation and idea that they won't which causes the pain.

When our expectations are not met and we feel angry or let down by a person or people, we often say something we will later regret. We can also have angry thoughts without saying anything, and these thoughts will continue to play over and over in our minds for hours and even days. And, boy, is that painful! Playing these thoughts over and over in our minds fires us up, and we either think about how we will reap our revenge or we feel sorry for ourselves and become really upset.

If we want peace and contentment, we have to learn to accept a simple fact: In our minds, people shouldn't, but in reality they do.

Our anger and disappointment is caused by our idea or society's idea. Projecting our ideas onto other people, however, brings pain. Sometimes what we are angry or disappointed about is morally or legally wrong. I understand that. But when our own ideas or expectations are causing us to be abusive and to be in conflict with another person, then we really have to take a step back and look at our thinking and behaviour. The reality of life is that people will always do things they shouldn't do.

Being angry or disappointed isn't going to change what other people do in life or what they have already done. All it does is destroy your peace of mind, darken your spirits, and end your relationships with family, friends, and partners.

We can find ourselves behaving like this towards our parents, especially when they have not treated us in the way we believe a parent should. But really, what did we know about being a parent? Did we go to parenting school? No, we didn't, yet we can get angry or disappointed with our parents because of our own idea of how a parent should behave. When we think like this, we start to feed those feelings by thinking about all of the things they should or shouldn't have done, and the more we remember, the more we convince ourselves that they are to blame for our feelings and negative behaviours.

We don't think about the fact that we have known our parents and family all of our lives and that we know their patterns of behaviour and what to expect from them. So when they have done something we believe they shouldn't have done, we should really be asking ourselves, 'What evidence do I have that I can expect anything different from them?'

But we don't, do we? Instead, we focus on what we believe they should have done for us and what they didn't do, instead of focusing on reality and what we know about them. Ask yourselves, 'What evidence do I have that someone will do what I am expecting them to do?' When we ask ourselves that question honestly, we find that we have no evidence.

Before they become parents, most people vow that they will spoil their own children, and give them all the things that they didn't have, and do all the things they wanted *their* parents to do for them. They believe that is what will make them better parents than their own parents were.

But it's a fact that every generation blames the one before for their mistakes in life. We've all heard others saying, 'If only my parents had done this or that, I wouldn't be in this mess.', 'They never loved me or knew how to show it.', 'It's their fault I turned out like this.' They believe they are victims, and can go through their entire lives blaming other people's behaviours and their past for what's going on in their own lives in the present.

We are not victims of life, my friends; we are victims of our imagination. In reality, we are survivors. We are still living and breathing, and if we want peace of mind and contentment, we have to stop thinking about what other people should have done or should be doing and begin to look at our own thinking and what *we* are doing. We are creating negative feelings by comparing reality with a picture we constructed in our mind; for we have no evidence other people are going to behave the way we imagine they should.

When the things we get angry or disappointed with are morally wrong, it hits a trigger. It's at that moment we must remember we have a choice: we can allow this to eat away at our spirit; or accept that just because people shouldn't, doesn't mean they won't. If we don't accept whatever it is that we are angry or disappointed with, it will fester in our minds and continue to cause us pain. Things play over and over in our minds because our spirit recognises that no matter what other people do, it's not spiritual to have hostile thoughts or behave badly towards others.

If something is playing over and over in our minds, we automatically think it's because whoever we are thinking about has done something wrong to us. Wrong! If something is playing over and over in our minds, it's because we are doing something which goes against the laws of spirit. It is because we are justifying our behaviour by focusing on what someone else has said or done.

We are not being true to our spirit. The blame and negative thoughts we are thinking are manifesting themselves as anger and disappointment. And the horrible sensations we are experiencing is our spirit either shaking or dying inside us, because we are not accepting that we are responsible for these feelings and that these feelings are caused by having our own ideas of how others should think and behave.

Unfortunately, in order for us to find peace, one of the things we have to accept in life is to admit to ourselves that our idea of how others should think and behave – our parents, partners, family members, friends, and people in general – is the cause of our unhappiness, anger, and disappointment. If we can accept that it is our idea that is causing the problem, we are ready for change. Instead of feeding our feelings with negative thoughts which then manifest into horrible sensations in our body, we will be taking responsibility for them. We can then feed our spirit with positivity, as we are now being honest with ourselves. When we do this, we will gradually find peace of mind and contentment, we will feel better about ourselves, and this will increase our self-esteem and confidence.

At first, it can be difficult. Because when you accept that it's your idea, something else will pop into your mind and you will be tempted to fall into a pattern of thinking you have used for a long time. Feeding the spirit isn't about who did what; it's about getting peace of mind and feeling contented, knowing you have done what is right for your spirit, and losing those feelings of anxiety because there was always something playing on your mind.

Only you can decide what you want to have the most: is it peace of mind, or the feelings of anger and disappointment? When you accept and take responsibility for the feelings you create, you learn to take control of your thinking, and you start to feel better about yourself and become more accepting of life and other people. This reduces the mental stress you have had on a daily and weekly basis, and the thoughts which have kept you trapped and caused unhappiness will leave you.

We can choose to learn from our experience, because it really is our greatest teacher. We can learn to challenge our negative thinking and recognise when we are thinking up ideas. When we do this, we are making spiritual progress which will bring us peace and contentment, or we can keep feeding our thoughts and be tormented by them for the rest of our lives.

People shouldn't but they do, and people will always do what they do because they see no wrong in what they do. So, do not interfere in things you have no power or control over, as it carries with it an enormous amount of pain and grief.

## Let's recap:

✦ There will always be something in life to challenge us. When we accept this and are grateful for the lesson, we will reap the reward.

✦ We are all the same. And when you finally accept this, you won't believe the peace you will feel.

✦ A valuable lesson on acceptance: people will always do as they do and it's none of our business. Accepting this through understanding and practising non-reaction brings so much joy, please believe me. Try and never take things personally, my friends. People are our teachers and earth is our training ground.

Not knowing or understanding anything about myself or life, but thinking that I did, nearly killed me.

The next chapter is all about our journey. A journey of self-discovery using our pain as our teacher and guide.

# Chapter Seven

## Go within or go without

Who am I, and why am I here? These are two questions I asked myself regularly when I was in pain. And believe me, I've experienced quite a bit of pain. The majority of my pain came through my expectations, my fears and ideas, along with my Catholic shame and guilt. To be rid of this shame and guilt, and the perception I had of the God I was raised with, was to be my biggest challenge.

Being controlled and conditioned within our homes and environments is one thing; being controlled and conditioned by someone else's beliefs is another. Back in the 1960s in Glasgow, I was told I had to go to Confession every Saturday night and to go to Mass every Sunday morning... or else. The 'or else' was a beating, no dinner, and told to stay in my room for a week. These were just a few of the conditions!

I was always confused as a child, and as an adult, about the God I was taught about. One week it was all fire and brimstone and an eye for an eye, and the following week it was all about how we should love one another. I would be told by my parents, grandparents, the priests, the school teachers, and anyone Catholic really, that if I was a bad boy I would go to hell and burn in the bad fire, and that I should be ashamed of myself for making mistakes. My whole life was based on the fear of a God I never knew or understood, and I ended up terrified, riddled with shame and guilt, and really insecure, because of what I was taught by others.

I had this picture in my mind of an old man with a long, grey beard, who lived in the sky somewhere that people called heaven, and he was waiting on me dying so he could judge me for my sins and then condemn me to the bad fire! It's funny now, but not so funny when you believe it. I don't blame anyone or my religion any more, but for years I did. I understand now that the people who said what they said were only repeating what they had learned from others, and obviously they thought that instilling the fear of God into your life was a normal thing to do.

That's what happened back in the 1960s, and for so many years I lived with this fear, shame, and guilt. And as we know by now, my friends, fear is the opposite of love. I used to think it was just me who carried this burden, but over the past 20 years or so, I have heard hundreds of people I have worked with share the same story.

The consequences of what we learn from others can be so detrimental to our growth. That's why awareness and understanding is so important; without them, we will only stay trapped in what we believe to be the norm. I cringe at times when I think of the fear I lived with for most of my life. The fear of a God I had never seen or experienced or understood, along with the fear of what others thought of me. My life was controlled by fear, and my fear then turned to anger and blame, and all because I knew nothing about myself, my life, or my purpose. All I knew about myself and life was what I had learned from other people, and some of the things I learned were to take me to the depths of insanity. But I know now that I had to go there to finally understand my own darkness. For when we are aware of our own fears and insecurities, we will also be aware of other people's. And that is a gift, if used out of love and not judgement.

I mentioned earlier that our own experiences are our greatest teachers in life, but unfortunately, we are not taught to learn from our mistakes and the emotional pain we go through. Instead, we have learned to punish ourselves and others, and to blame rather than to be responsible, which is why it is so difficult to break these old habits. Not knowing or understanding anything about life or ourselves is where all the pain comes from. And, if we are honest, we all look for things on the outside to make us feel good on the inside. It's difficult to change something you have been doing over a period of time, because for years and years you found nothing wrong with it. We even believed the emotional pain and suffering we have gone through was normal, but we now know that it's far from normal.

What is normal anyway? Comfort zones are normal; they are called comfort zones because this is where we feel the most comfortable. We are safe in our own cocoon with all our needs, and some people cannot wait to get back to that each day! Normal hurts, as we all know, and that's why we get agitated at times and feel uneasy within ourselves because our soul is crying out for change. When someone is at total peace within themselves and they are living their life without fear or worry, we see that as strange. To be honest, we see anything outwith the norm as strange, don't we?

Getting to know your true self can be scary, as can admitting to yourself that you have been wrong at times. But as soon as you decide you have had enough pain and are willing to change, the peace comes flowing in. Most people think and believe that change is impossible, but please believe me, it's not. Our own experience tells us we need to change, our pain and sorrow tells us, our spirit tells us – and hopefully this book tells you – that some of the behaviours we have learned and the negative way that we have learned to think, are hurtful and unhealthy, and the only way for us to find true peace is through change.

Changing my perception of God and my old belief system was difficult, due to the fear I carried within me, but I knew I couldn't continue to fear this old man any more. I was so scared to change my perception, but the shame and guilt was getting too much and too deep within me and I knew I had to do something. Then one day in 1995, whilst in Rehab recovering from drug and alcohol misuse, my whole perception changed.

I had a spiritual experience when I received the news that my grandmother had passed away. Not at that precise moment, but about 15 minutes later when I went to my room, locked my door, and began to think about suicide. You see, my grandmother was my best friend and someone I loved dearly, so when I heard the news of her death I just wanted to die, too.

But life is about experiences. The experience I had that day when I received the news about my grandmother was to change my entire life. And through that and other experiences, I now know and understand myself and my creator. I also know and understand how difficult it is to believe someone when you haven't experienced what they have experienced, but when we open our minds and our hearts, believe me, you will experience unconditional love.

On the day I received the news about my grandmother's passing, I was thinking about leaving the Rehab to score drugs and then ending my life, but by the time I had finished my last negative sentence, something weird happened. I say weird because I had never experienced a feeling of total peace and calmness like this before. I felt as if my grandmother was sitting beside me on the bed. I couldn't see her, but I felt her, and I heard her say to me that she was ok and that she was with me now.

My tears stopped, and I felt as if I was as light as a feather. All the pain I had imagined would happen, never occurred; I was absent of all fear. I know now that I was living in the moment, as my mind was totally quiet and the feeling I experienced can only be described as peaceful. I'm smiling now as I remember how I used to laugh and criticise people when they told me of their spiritual experiences, but in those days I was ignorant, closed-minded, arrogant, a total doubter, and stubborn.

Please believe me, I have no reason to lie. Everything you have read and are going to read comes from lived experiences, and Lorraine and I share our experiences so that others may find the identification they need in order to change and find peace. Our goal is to pass on what we have learned so that others can break the cycle of dysfunction within their own lives, and in doing this become powerful examples for others to follow.

The spiritual experience had also awakened the spirit within me, and I began to think more positively and to look at changing my career. Until then, really all I had done was labour, lie, and steal. Oh yes, and take drugs and alcohol on a daily basis! So, I decided I wanted to become a therapist/counsellor, and for once I really meant it. And that's exactly what I did when I left the treatment centre four months later.

This was to be the beginning of my new journey, and I was excited that I had experienced what man called God. I had felt a peace like never before… without any mind-altering chemicals! The difference this time was that the power came from within, and that's when I finally realised that I was spirit as well as human. My grandmother always told me when I was young that the kingdom of heaven lies within us, seek and you shall find, and that we are spiritual beings having human experiences.

Now I finally began to understand what she meant. Well, just a little! My perception of God and this old scary man in heaven had finally changed, and I felt happy for the first time in a long time. But that was all to change, as work was about to begin.

Earth is our training ground and people are our teachers, and this was to be the beginning of my training. It was strange, because although I felt fear in leaving the Rehab, I never once felt like using alcohol or drugs again. I felt as though my grandmother was with me, and I think that believing this helped me in dealing with my fears. It's difficult to explain, really, for although there was anxiety and fear at times, it was nothing like it had been before. And I do know that was down to my gratitude; nothing more and nothing less.

I had never been grateful for anything in my whole entire life. And when I found gratitude, I realised why I was so miserable, angry, and unhappy at times. Gratitude is the king of all virtues, my friends, for when we are grateful we are connected to the light, and no darkness, pain or worry can touch us – and that's a promise.

I was so grateful that I had had that experience, and totally grateful to be free from drugs and alcohol. My mental health problems were gone, and for once I felt good within myself. That's why I know that gratitude is good for the spirit and can bring healing and peace.

A fortnight after I left the treatment centre, I was walking around the city centre in Glasgow. On the other side of the road I saw this big red door with a sign: Community service volunteers. So I went over and knocked on the door, and met this lovely woman called Pat, who sat me down with a cup of tea and listened to my story. She was amazed, and that same day she took me to a project in Possilpark, Glasgow, where I spoke with some of the staff and management. The charity was called Fairbridge, who work with disadvantaged young people who have very similar upbringings and experiences as myself. The next day, I was working as a volunteer. Now, who would ever have thought that would happen?

The manager and staff were amazing and extremely supportive, and for the first time in a long time I felt part of something. I felt loved, and for once I felt worthy. And believe me, it was just at the right time. Later that week, I received news that my father had passed away suddenly, and not long after that my youngest sister died. On both these occasions, I felt the same peace, because I truly believed they were with me, and that's down to the experience I had with my grandmother. Yes, I cried, but not out of self-pity. I cried because I missed them, but I also had a strong faith and a belief that they were with me and that they were going to help and guide me. And I really and truly believed this. The way I looked at it was I had three angels at my side, and this comforted me and helped me to get through my days, as I was always talking to them. I still do, along with all my family and friends who have passed over to spirit.

Having this new way of thinking and believing, along with my gratitude, changed my life around. Jack, who was the manager at Fairbridge, was incredible. He really took to me, and helped me with my career. He sent me to an elderly lady who taught me how to read and write at the age of 35, which boosted my confidence immensely. He then found the money to send me on training courses, then driving lessons, then college and university, and within 18 months I had learned to read and write, passed my driving test, and completed my counselling courses. He also showed me how to raise money for my Diploma, and encouraged me to go and do something with my life, which I did six months later.

I am so grateful to Jack and all the staff at Fairbridge who were there for me at the beginning of my journey, and I will never forget the love, support, and guidance they gave me. Four years later, I was living the dream – and I thought nothing could go wrong. I had passed my Diploma in Counselling and Supervision, had built up a very good CV, had my own house, my own car, savings in the bank, and a good reputation.

So, what could possibly go wrong? Well, everything really.

Throughout those four years, I had gratitude every single day... until one day I lost it, and that's when the pain came tumbling back into my life. Everything you have read so far within this book, I have also experienced, my friends: the dysfunctional learned behaviours; the habits and negative reactions; the terrible fears which control us; the negative feelings and emotions; the anger, blame, resentments, etc. And that's why it's so important to share our experiences of being able to come through such emotional pain, so that we can help others to break this horrid cycle of dysfunction.

During that four years, I had barely looked at myself. I was always busy working, going to meetings and volunteering, but this was to stop. I started to search and look for more knowledge, and I began to read the Bible and other religious and spiritual books.

I hadn't had any other spiritual experiences since my family passed over, and I wanted more. I knew there was something out there, and I wanted to know what it was. Big, big mistake on my part! I knew nothing, but thought I knew everything. I wasn't aware of my ego; in fact, the pain I was to go through again, along with the fear, shame, and guilt, came from me thinking I was special. I really believed that the spiritual experiences I'd had when my family passed over made me different from others; another big mistake on my part.

When I lost my gratitude, I also lost my trust and faith, and I began to question and doubt my own experiences. I allowed fear back into my life, and my ego was in total control. I had no defence, because I didn't know then what I know now. And to top it all off, I had fallen out with my new God. I can laugh now at how immature I was. I began to get angry and annoyed with this new God and my family for not helping me out! Basically, for not giving me what I wanted.

You see, I couldn't recognise, nor was I aware, that what I had read within the beautiful spiritual books, I was also expecting to happen to me. I knew deep down I was spirit because of what happened to me when my family passed away, and because all the books I had read were telling me how powerful I was, how much I was loved, and all the great things I could do. And that is all true... But I expected everything to happen overnight. I expected to always be free of pain, to have my own Rehab one day, my nice cottage, my work accredited, and my books to be best sellers. My ego and grandiosity were on top form and I couldn't even see it coming. I got so caught up in ME that I forgot my primary purpose, and that was to help others to be free from pain.

Now I felt like a complete hypocrite, and the fear, shame, and guilt came back with a vengeance. All the old behaviours crept back in, and it didn't matter how many qualifications I had or how many religious and spiritual books I had read, if you don't know how to change and you have no mental or spiritual defence, then you will struggle. Knowledge is worthless without action and faith, and at this point of my journey I had lost both – and my ego was in control. I had no awareness or understanding; all the books I had read and all my qualifications had not prepared me for this onslaught of darkness.

My studies meant nothing to me at this point, as they hadn't shown me how to change or how to deal with these horrible feelings and emotions. All I did was to keep praying and praying for something to happen, in the same way I had when I was a child or in trouble. I was hoping for some miracle to happen, maybe my grandmother or an angel to appear and tell me it was just a dream. Well, that's what my mind was hoping for!

I reverted to the old man in the sky God, and felt as if I was being punished. And this pattern of behaviour was to go on for years. It was during this dark period that I realised I was a total hypocrite and was walking about with a mask on. I was training people from organisations on how to deal with anger and stress, plus I was supporting people with addiction and mental health problems within and outwith my community, but the shame and guilt I felt for being paid good money for this almost crippled me.

When things aren't sitting right with us, my friends, our spirit is showing us we need to change something, and we need to be responsible. But I didn't know that then, and that's why I was in so much pain. I was also in a relationship and about to get married, but I had to end it as I was all over the place. And the shame and guilt I felt for ending it didn't help matters. I became so angry with myself and my belief system that I wanted to end my life. I became aggressive again, as I was controlled by fear, and I blamed it all on this old man in the sky. I began to isolate myself and wear my mask when I went out of the house. Privately, I was totally ashamed and felt terrible guilt as I knew I had lost my gratitude, and the reason I had lost my gratitude was because I had gone searching for more knowledge. I had completely forgotten about my earlier journey and the things that had been given to me.

I wasn't grateful for what I had any more; I never practised change, as I didn't know how to; and I felt I didn't need to after the experiences I'd had when my family passed over. Nor did I put the action in that is required in order to change. I thought I knew myself and my creator, but all I knew was words. I reverted back to the old Gerard, as that was all I knew. I behaved like a spoilt child when I couldn't get what I expected from this God, and regularly threw a tantrum. I wanted more, and wanting more without knowing or understanding why I wanted it was the cause of my pain, despite the beautiful spiritual experiences I'd had.

And the moral of the story, my friends, is that it doesn't matter how many qualifications we have, or how many books we have read, or how much faith we think we have. Unless we truly understand what's happening to us and why it is happening, we will always be guessing, blaming, expecting, and hurting, until we finally decide that our way of thinking, behaving, and living needs changing.

## Beginning to understand, and learning from our pain

My heart was broken, and I continued to punish myself through the shame and guilt of letting my family in spirit down as well as this God I was trying to get to know. I soon found out that freedom from emotional pain doesn't come from knowing everything; it comes from letting go from wanting to know everything. It had taken me years to learn from my mistakes and also to learn that mistakes are there for us to learn from; they're not there for us to punish ourselves.

When we make a mistake while we are writing, we rub it out, re-think, and start again. And life's exactly the same. We have to dust ourselves down, pick ourselves up, learn from the pain, and continue on our journey. Only this time, we have to be truly grateful for the pain and the experience, because the Universe is only trying to strengthen us by pointing out our defects of character. For your true character is spirit, and spirit is love. And when we are in pain, we do not love. We have to be able to recognise what we are doing that is preventing us from feeling unconditional love, and learn to take responsibility for it. For this is our life, our minds, and our spirit. And, sorry to say it again, but we are responsible for all three.

It was only when I met Lorraine that I began to understand more about myself, especially the learned behaviours and expectations. But learning from Lorraine was also difficult, because my ego was still hanging around. Although she taught me loads, it was still down to me to put the work in, and the first thing for me to do was to swallow my pride, surrender, and learn humility. And again, I found this very difficult.

I fought with Lorraine for years because of my pride and ego, and for years she stuck by me. Eventually the penny began to drop that change takes time and getting to know your true self takes courage, but I wanted it to happen while I was sleeping! I didn't want to put the work in. I wanted this God I had pictured to give me everything on a plate because of all the people I had helped and supported, plus all the voluntary work, sacrifices, and pain I had gone through. And I truly believed I was entitled to it.

I knew nothing and understood nothing, but because I had read a few books, had qualifications and had a few spiritual experiences, I thought I knew everything. I thought I was special and that I was going to change the world, when really, I couldn't change my own thinking. All the anger, fear, blame, guilt, and shame took its toll on me and on my body, as I explained earlier. I went to the doctors, but all they knew about the body and its pain came from science and what they had studied and learned at university and from books.

They can only diagnose and prescribe, as this is what they have learned. They are not aware or taught about the spirit; it's only lately that scientists and spiritualists have begun working together. For years, scientists dismissed that there was something powerful out there, and for years I just went with what the doctors said. I'm not saying they are wrong, not by any means. They work with the body, but it's the mind and all those horrid negative thoughts that do the damage to our bodies and spirit.

The reason I know this is through my own experience, and over 23 years observing people healing themselves through learning to take responsibility for the behaviour which is causing their pain. There have been hundreds of thousands of spiritual books written about who we are, why we are here, and what we are responsible for; some selling millions of copies worldwide. There are also many people throughout the years who have inspired others by the profound changes they have made within their own lives. These changes and all these books came through people learning from their mistakes and their pain, and that's why the books sold in their millions. People find identification through other people's experiences, which in turn helps them to identify what they are experiencing within their own lives.

Through this identification, along with having the awareness and understanding, change can begin. Certain people throughout the centuries – like us – thought they could never change, but have inspired and motivated us because they learned from their mistakes and found inner peace through getting to know themselves and their creator.

It was their own experiences which taught them what they know, and it's the same with us. My journey began when I left Rehab, and I had to experience what I did or else I wouldn't have continued on this path or been able to write this book and do the work I do. I had to search and go through the pain in order for me to understand that life is all about learning, and my spiritual journey is about un-learning all the negative things I learned as a child – the negative thoughts, behaviours, and expectations which prevented me from loving myself and others.

This was to be my job now. My paid work I was to treat as a hobby and be grateful for it, as it was paying my bills, and feeding me, and keeping a roof over my head. But my main job was to unlearn all those negative behaviours Lorraine and I have written about. It had taken nearly 15 years of searching and hurting before I began to build a relationship with myself and my higher power, and that only came about because I ended up in hospital. That was the day I cried my eyes out as I was shown how selfish, arrogant, ungrateful, and egotistical I had become.

It was also the day I decided I'd had enough pain. I gave up my work as a consultant because I was a hypocrite, and I took up hill walking and photography for the next three years. In that time, I began to appreciate life and nature more, whilst learning about myself and what's written within this book.

I began to practise quieting my mind whilst I was out walking, and practised Tai-Chi and meditation. I remembered that while I had been in Rehab, my grandmother had only been able to speak to me when my mind was quiet. It was in doing these activities that I finally realised that we are energy, and very powerful energy at that. This time I had finally surrendered to my way of thinking, and this time I felt the love. Sometimes I would be blessed in meditation and get to see images of my family and friends and feel their presence, and this comforted me knowing that I wasn't alone. It also helped to restore my faith.

Faith is blind, and to trust in a power greater than ourselves can be extremely difficult, especially when you can't see, hear, or feel this power, and all you really know about it came from other people, books, and your imagination. But I had experienced this power years earlier, as I've explained, and had been on an amazing journey for four years where nothing had gone wrong – because I was full of gratitude. Then one day, because I never got what I wanted when I wanted it, I had begun to doubt. I then paid the price for not knowing or understanding but thinking I knew everything, when all I was doing was listening to my ego, the voice of lies.

To listen to our spirit, which is our conscience, our mind has to be quiet. You might have to tell your mind to shut up! It really depends on how much peace you want within your life, and how much practice you're willing to put into being at peace with yourself.

I finally began to understand myself and what life is about when I stopped searching and began to be grateful again. Learning humility was difficult, but so is change. And the more practice you put in, the greater the rewards.

I really did think when I left Rehab that I had surrendered to God's will, but I never knew God or His will – and still don't. I have experienced severe pain, and also total peace and serenity, but I have never met God. I have been fortunate enough to see some beautiful things through meditation, including glimpses of my family, and I have experienced an amazing, loving, healing energy, but I've never met the old man in the sky yet!

We all have our own perception of a god, and I'm certainly not going to try and influence you to change that perception. We either choose to believe or we don't, and that's a choice we all have. My experience and understanding today, if it helps anyone, is that we are all spiritual beings as well as human. Our body is the vehicle which carries the spirit, and spirit is who we really are. Our spirit is also our teacher, guide, and healer. And when we are living in fear and misbehaving, our body and spirit hurts – as we have already experienced; but when we are thinking and behaving in a loving and caring manner, we feel the loving energy within us. This is something we have all experienced, but what we have learned prevents us from finding out the truth.

I always believed there was something out there, and still do, but I went searching for it in the wrong places. I have read many a book in my time, watched documentaries, studied all religions, astrology, numerology, and listened to many spiritual people speaking on YouTube, but it was my own pain and my own mistakes and my own experiences that brought me to the light. I learned to tap into this energy through practising change and opening my mind.

I remember thinking one day, 'What was it you were looking and searching for anyway?' And that's when I began to laugh. My grandmother and the books were right: the kingdom of heaven does lie within us, but I was seeking it in the wrong places. I wanted to please this God in the same way as I wanted to please other people, because I had never known how to love. I couldn't see the lessons the Universe was trying to show me, due to my ignorance and self-will, but I know now that I just wasn't ready. I wasn't ready to go out and help people because I couldn't help myself; I was full of ego and fear, and basically knew nothing about life even though I thought I did.

That was me seeking, and what I found I didn't like. And usually what I didn't like was the truth. As we all know by now, the truth hurts. But the truth will also set us free from the lies we have been telling ourselves, once we find the courage to face it.

You have nothing to fear any more, my friends. Having read this far, you now understand fear, and the more you begin to believe in yourself, the happier and more confident you will become.

Like most people, I wanted to be comfortable within my own skin, but that's easier said than done. I was tired of people saying, 'Just be still. Breathe slowly. Let it go. It will pass. Just hand it over to God.' I didn't want to hear that. I wanted the pain to go away and never come back again, but that was impossible because I was always blaming. I understand now why people blame and fear this God we all talk about, because I did it myself.

I also understand the pain behind losing a loved one, and how easy it is to blame this God. It's the same with disasters, murders, famine and drought, addictions, suicides, war, diseases and illnesses. You hear people, including me, saying, 'How can this God allow this to happen?' Yet none of us has met this God, but we speak as if we know Him personally.

I've never met God, but I've experienced peace and love through doing what I believe to be right, and my experience tells me that it's man's own doing that brings the pain and suffering going on throughout the world. For example, we take things from the ground when centuries ago we were told not to. We dig for gold, silver, diamonds, rubies, coal, oil and gas, etc, and we have been doing it for decades, then we wonder what's happening to our planet and why disasters occur. Throughout the centuries, and still to this present day, people have been killing in the name of God, as if they knew Him. Every day, children die through starvation and thirst and millions are living in poverty; it's been going on for centuries, and still man continues to allow it to happen in the 21st century.

There's people and children being raped and sexually assaulted daily throughout the world, and tens of thousands being murdered, and it's people who are doing it. We torture one another; we hate one another; we think we are better than others; we take what we want; and some do what they want. But it's never man's fault. It's always this God that we think we know who gets the blame.

It might have taken me a while to open my mind and my heart, but I understand more about myself, the Universe, and this God we all talk about now than I ever did before. And I only know this since I stopped questioning everything. As I get older, I'm becoming more teachable. So, you never know what's around the corner. I could still get to see this God before I pass!

It's true that we never know what lies ahead of us and we never know when our time here on earth is up. So, please enjoy each moment and do the things you thought you could never do. I know there's a power out there which also lives within us, because I've experienced it. I do not know God, but I do know that the things that have been revealed to me and the beautiful things that have happened to me could only have come from a loving, compassionate, powerful source which man calls God.

I'm pretty sure you will experience this power and energy yourself; probably many of you have already. It was learning to find the balance between mind, body, and spirit, and keeping the connection with this power, that I found challenging – but also very rewarding – when I began to understand life a little more. It's new, and everything new is difficult at the beginning. But with practice we get better, stronger, and more confident.

Try to remember that pain and mistakes are there to help us on our journey, and that's why we have them. If we can't learn from them there and then, the Universe will send them back to us until we do. That's why we are faced with the same problems year in and year out, for what goes around comes around and it will always be that way until we learn the lessons the Universe is trying to teach us. Sadly, because we know nothing about ourselves, life, or its purpose, we just continue to live in a life of total chaos, confusion, and dysfunction.

I gave up looking for answers and knowledge, and I found peace. I found it through learning to take responsibility for my own mistakes and my own pain, and not interfering in other people's business. We all have our own journey, and I have learned through my experience not to interfere in another person's travels unless I am invited along. Interfering and enabling someone on their journey is only preventing them from learning what they themselves are responsible for. Sometimes advice-giving and interference can also be damaging to their spirit and can prevent them from learning. That's why it's best to lead by example and not by our egos. Learn to live your life your way, and allow others to do the same. This way, you will find great peace.

I know I am spirit now as well as human, and I know I am here to learn about love. How to find it, how to feel it, and how to share it. I also believe in a power greater than myself; a power of unconditional love that works through us, is always with us, and always trying to guide us back to the innocence of the child. But the things that we learned whilst growing up within our homes and environments have prevented this from happening, and that's why most of us go searching.

This is what I now understand and believe about myself and life. This is what my pain and searching has taught me; to keep it very simple, to go with the flow of life, and not to fight against it. To accept my past and learn from its mistakes, as my past is my greatest asset. To always be grateful for the simple things in life and never forget that gratitude is the king of all virtues. For when we are full of gratitude, we will also be blessed with unconditional love.

Mind, body, and spirit, my friends, that's what we are responsible for; nothing more and nothing less. And when we are in control of all three, we are not only living in peace but we are also connected to that source of powerful, positive, loving energy which man calls God.

## Mind, body, and spirit

Taking care of our own minds and being watchful over our own thoughts and the words we use is our responsibility. Learning to quiet our minds, through whatever practice you find works for you, is how you will learn to listen to your spirit and its guidance. And through practice you will find an inner peace like never before. The mind is very powerful, as you have already experienced; it can make us and break us, and that's why it's so important we look after it. For when we let our mind go, we also let our bodies go and our spirit dies within.

When we are thinking negatively or we are living in fear, we can easily neglect our bodies and our spirits. We forget that we have only one body and that we are responsible for its upkeep. We are responsible for keeping it clean on a regular basis, or else it will smell. We are also responsible for what we put into our bodies; if we eat healthy foods and take responsibility for what we eat, our bodies will always stay healthy; if we choose to eat unhealthy foods, which we tend to do when we are upset, lazy, stressed-out, angry or depressed, our bodies die along with our spirit. Having a healthy body comes down to having a healthy mind. It's really that simple, but our complicated minds won't allow us to process that straightforward information.

Our bodies also need exercise so that we can keep fit and enjoy our lives to the full. Self-discipline and self-control are what we require. If we allow our negative thoughts to control us and we neglect our bodies, it's not just the poor hygiene and smell, obesity, or anorexia we need to worry about, it's the physical, emotional, and spiritual pain, too.

The physical, emotional, and spiritual pain comes from not feeding our spirit with love, in my experience. And it's something I have also experienced whilst working with others throughout the years. People who struggle with mental health problems can't recognise what they are doing to themselves. When I put weight on, I justified it and used excuses, but deep down I loathed myself. It was the same when I wasn't eating; I looked and felt terrible. I wasn't aware that my negative thinking and moods were the cause of my unhealthy eating habits, probably because I didn't care. The mind can control us, or we can control our minds. Hopefully, you are aware of this now.

Throughout the book we have looked at what our minds can do to us, due to our lack of awareness and understanding. We suffer because we don't know, but hopefully now that the scientists are working alongside the spiritualists, great changes will come about. We also hope that what you have read within these pages will help you to do great things, but first you have to learn about what we are responsible for and why we are responsible for it. Finding the balance is the key, and that balance will come through not wanting to hurt any more.

Now you have the awareness and understanding, all we need to do is to sort out your lazy mind!

Whatever is going on within our minds is how our bodies and spirits will feel. When our mind becomes lazy, we also become lazy, and that can be dangerous. Laziness of the mind can cause accidents and some of these can be dangerous, even life-threatening, due to a lack of concentration or thinking about something else. When we are feeling down and our spirits are dead, it's because our egos are having a party within our minds, and we just sit there on our pity stools enjoying the self-pity party, listening to our egos, not knowing or understanding that we are responsible for these feelings and emotions. This is unhealthy and dangerous, and it prevents us from learning and living.

Laziness of the mind comes from not being aware, not being vigilant around our own thinking, and allowing complacency to enter into our lives. And before we know it, we have formed comfort zones which, as we all know by now, prevent us from living. We can sit there and justify all we like, but deep down we know we can really dislike ourselves, hate ourselves, and loathe ourselves when we stop taking care of ourselves.

Take care of your mind, practise being absent of all negative thoughts, teach yourself to quieten your mind by not answering it back, and please try to always be positive and grateful. In doing this, you will find that your body and spirit will follow. Wash regularly, exercise when you can, watch what you are eating, and practise being kind to yourself. For when we are feeding our spirits with love, gratitude, positivity, and thanksgiving, our bodies will also reap the rewards. I'm not talking about the world's strongest man here, or the body of a catwalk model! All I'm saying is that if you want to live a long and healthy life without any regrets or pain, then you must take responsibility for your own mind, body, and spirit.

Scientists have commented lately that obesity could be down to a gene of some sort, but when I heard this I was gobsmacked that educated people could come up with such a statement. Did it just appear? I work with people who are obese, and I listen to them week in and week out. I can see how unhappy and depressed they really are because of the shame, guilt, and regret they carry around with them.

I was also obese at one point in my life, and when I share my experiences with others who are suffering from obesity, they find immediate identification with the thoughts, feelings, and behaviours that led to me putting on so much weight in the first place. But if I look back at my childhood, I realise that few people were obese in my day or before it. Maybe it was because in the 60s and 70s we never had much, and what we did have we were entirely grateful for. The guys played football straight after school, or went jumping dykes, or raking household bins looking for a lucky one, and basically getting up to no good, while the girls played skipping, hopscotch, or throwing old tennis balls against the wall and catching them. Our parents had to shout out of the window or send someone to find us and let us know that our dinner was ready. Back then, a lot more children were fit and healthy, because we were out playing no matter the weather and we always had cooked meals. We never had your burger joints or curry takeaways, and we never had the pound shops or shopping centres selling chocolate, crisps, and sugary things very cheaply.

We never had home delivery either! Our mothers went for their own shopping, but today you can have your food and meals delivered directly to your house. Most people today sit at home anyway; they're either playing games on computers, or they're on social media telling everyone their problems, blaming others, gossiping, or showing off their dinner! I have nearly knocked down at least six people because they were too busy looking at their phones rather than the red traffic light at a road junction! How things have changed over the years!

Since we are talking about obesity and laziness of the mind, I thought I would share this jokey piece that I was sent, and I would like to thank whoever it was who wrote it. It basically explains the differences from my day to the present day, and will probably appeal to those of you over the age of 40!

*Now that I'm over the ripe old age of forty, I can't help but look around and notice the youth of today. You've got it so easy! I mean, compared to my childhood, you live in a UTOPIA! And I hate to say it, but you kids today, you don't know how good you've got it!*

*I mean, when I was a kid we didn't have the Internet. If we wanted to know something, we had to go to the bloody library and look it up ourselves, in the card catalogue!!*

*There was no email!! We had to actually write somebody a letter – with a pen! Then you had to walk all the way across the street and put it in the mailbox and it would take, like, a week to get there! Stamps were 5 pence!*

*Child Protective Services didn't care if our parents beat us. As a matter of fact, the parents of all my friends also had permission to kick the shit out of us! Nowhere was safe!*

*There were no MP3s or Napsters! If you wanted to steal music, you had to hitchhike to the record store and shoplift it yourself! Or you had to wait around all day to tape it off the radio, and the DJ would usually talk over the beginning and f..k it all up! There were no CD players! We had tape decks in our car. We'd play our favourite tape and 'eject' it when finished and the tape would come undone. Cos that's how we rolled, dig?*

*We didn't have fancy crap like Call Waiting! If you were on the phone and somebody else called, they got a busy signal, that's it!*

*And we didn't have fancy Caller ID either! When the phone rang, you had no idea who it was! It could be your school, your mum, your boss, your bookie, your drug dealer, a collections agent, you just didn't know!!! You had to pick it up and take your chances, mister!*

*We didn't have any fancy Sony PlayStation video games with high-resolution 3D graphics! We had the Atari 2600! With games like 'Space Invaders' and 'Asteroids'. Your guy was a little square! You actually had to use your imagination!! And there were no multiple levels or screens; it was just one screen... forever! And you could never win. The game just kept getting harder and harder and faster and faster until you died! Just like LIFE!*

*You had to use a little book called a TV Guide to find out what was on! You were screwed when it came to channel surfing! You had to get off your ass and walk over to the TV to change the channel! NO REMOTES!!!*

*There was no Cartoon Network either! You could only get cartoons on a Saturday morning. Do you hear what I'm saying?! We had to wait ALL WEEK for cartoons!!*

*And we didn't have microwaves; if we wanted to heat something up, we had to use the cooker! Imagine that! That's exactly what I'm talking about! You kids today have got it too easy. You're spoiled. You little grunts wouldn't have lasted five minutes back in the 1970s or before!*

*Regards, Grumpy Gang.*

I laughed my head off when I read this as it's so true, and it fits in with what I've been talking about. People have everything at their fingertips now, and today's generation has it so easy – but it's not their fault; it's part of evolution, and this is their journey now and not ours. The past cannot be changed, my friends, it can only be learned from. And I'm hoping the scientists begin to learn that the message they are portraying about a gene being responsible for obesity is wrong for them to say. They have no evidence, and their message can be harmful to those who are suffering from this condition, because they can now use this gene as an excuse for their obesity. And if they do that, they will never be able to take responsibility for their eating habits, their health, or the negative thoughts that are running through their minds on a daily basis. Responsibility will be taken away from them, and they will have something else to blame or use as an excuse for their condition.

I have yet to meet anyone who is totally happy and comfortable with their obesity. If you were to listen to the stories I have heard, you will find that most sufferers despise themselves, and live with fear, shame, guilt, and regret. They feel their personal hygiene becomes neglected, their faces and bodies change, their confidence, self-worth, and self-esteem are lost, their sex life and their relationships with people are nil, their health is poorly, and any goodness they had within them has been lost. They feel they can't go to places they used to frequent, and many will remain housebound due to their health or their fears.

People really do think they understand other people, when really we don't even understand ourselves. When we let our minds go, we also let our bodies go, and when this happens we have no defence against the dark because our spirit is also dead. There is no positivity or hope within us, and we can't see the lesson the Universe is trying to show us. We eat on our feelings and emotions, we drink, take drugs, gamble, and run away from them, because we do not know ourselves, nor do we know what happened to us and why it happened. But your own experience is your greatest teacher, and when you learn from it, you can then pass it onto others.

The present UK government is in the same frame of mind when it comes to addiction, blaming the alcohol for the amount of alcoholism within the country, and believing that putting the price of alcohol up and selling it at different times of the day will prevent or reduce alcoholism and the number of deaths. They did the same thing with tobacco; they increased the prices dramatically in order to reduce the amount of deaths which they believed were caused through smoking. But they don't understand that the alcohol and the tobacco are not the problems. The majority of people who are obese, drink heavily, smoke heavily, or seriously abuse drugs, also suffer from mental health problems. And the only way these people know how to deal with the thoughts, feelings, and emotions they experience on a daily basis, is to take the drug of their choice. That's what they believe is their medicine.

Trying to control people will never work; it never has and it never will. We talk about this in earlier chapters and throughout the book: thinking is the king of all addictions, and that's why society will always struggle because it fails to recognise this.

Science, putting prices up, and trying to control people, won't change them or help them to live longer. Scientists and heads of governments are only human, and humans make mistakes. They guess and make assumptions the same as we do, and they think they know what's best for others, just as we do. They have egos, the same as us, they hurt the same as us, and hopefully they can learn from their mistakes the same as us!

Throughout the centuries, science has made some incredible and amazing breakthroughs to sustain life, as have many doctors and other professionals who work within this field. But sadly, reality shows us that addiction and mental health is rife throughout the world, the same as crime. Our hospitals and prisons are full, unemployment is at its highest, and the suicide rates are still increasing. So really, something has got to change, because no-one seems to know who they are and what they are responsible for.

Love is missing, and we all know that. This book explains the things that prevent us from showing and feeling love, but hopefully it will also teach you how to show and feel it through becoming aware and understanding that we are love. Millions have healed themselves throughout the centuries by changing their thinking, their behaviours, and their old beliefs. Some experienced wake-up calls, others had spiritual awakenings, some used their pain, whilst others already knew and believed that they could heal themselves. Because we can't see spirit, we deny it and doubt it, and this has been man's problem for centuries – me included. Coming to believe in who you really are and experiencing the power and love within you, will come through your own experience – and that's a promise.

## Let's recap:

You will experience all the positive, spiritual things that we have written about within these pages once you learn that you alone are responsible for your own mind, body, and spirit. Never quit, never give up; your awareness and your body will always keep you centered. Always look within, and never forget whose in control.

# Chapter Eight

## No more fear, no more pain

### Panic and anxiety attacks

Panic and anxiety attacks are two things which really frightened me. When I experienced them, I really thought at times I was going to die. Not understanding the cause of my anxiety and panic attacks kept me trapped for years. I experienced them on a regular basis, and anyone who has experienced them will know what I'm talking about. The overwhelming feeling of fear that passes through our bodies causes us to panic or feel anxious, and when we are in a full blown attack it becomes very frightening. What we see, what we hear, what we touch, taste, and smell, as well as what we tell ourselves – they are all triggers that can set off an attack. Try and remember this. The reaction to sight, sound, and what we tell ourselves chapter should also help with your awareness.

Everyone has experienced trauma at some point in their lives, just as everyone has panicked and felt anxious at times. It's fair to say that some of us are stronger than others when it comes to dealing with these things, but it's unfair to think that just because we can deal with them, others should be able to as well.

This is where empathy comes in handy. Empathy is simply putting yourself in the other person's shoes and trying to understand how they must feel when they are faced with an attack. We panic and become anxious because we have allowed fear to enter our lives, and within seconds our thinking changes and we begin to gather false evidence. What we are telling ourselves within that moment is causing us to panic and feel anxious, and we do this out of habit.

Take starting school as an example. Some kids love it and can't wait to get to school, but others don't and they cry their little eyes out, panic, become anxious, and struggle to breathe. Leaving their parents behind and being with total strangers frightens them, and they begin to panic as this experience is something new to them. They are only children, my friends, and they are not aware of their fears or why they panic and feel anxious. But because they are not being taught to understand why they are feeling this way, it often becomes a pattern of behaviour that they will carry with them throughout their lives. Teachers and parents will try their best to show love and compassion, but unless we understand why it is happening to us and why we are feeling this way, then how else can we change it? That is the case for innocent children of five years of age, but most grown-up adults still don't understand! Fear has so many disguises, and it is so cunning that it can overwhelm us to the point where we begin to feel anxious and panic.

Another example. You go to the cash machine one day, and when the balance appears on the screen it's not what you expected. You panic and become anxious, and within seconds a deluge of negative thoughts comes rushing in. The first of these thoughts is usually OMG! The fear of not having enough money, or not having *any* money, has caused you to panic and feel anxious again, because this probably won't have been the first time that this has happened – and it won't be the last.

We can't see that the lesson the Universe is trying to teach us is that we are financially insecure. And if we can't see the lesson, then we will continue to panic and feel anxious every time our finances are low. Are we being greedy? Are we living by our needs or are we living by our wants? Are we worshipping money? Are we selfish and ungrateful? Are we lazy? Ask yourself: 'Why am I feeling anxious, and why am I beginning to panic?'

Think of a time when you have told a lie and it has come back to bite you, or you have done something you know you shouldn't have done and you have been found out. Can you remember how you felt? Do you remember panicking, and the horrible anxiety you felt when you found out that you were going to be confronted for your lies or your dishonesty? Can you remember the feelings within your body, and your head racing a hundred miles an hour trying to think of more lies to tell to get yourself out of the mess?

Then ask yourself, 'How many times do I have to go through this process before I learn the lesson? How many times have I ended up in this position?' If you have done something you know you shouldn't have done, then be ready for your karma; if you have lied for your own selfish gain, then also be prepared for your karma. For what goes around comes around, so try and remember this. And the next time you find yourself in this position, ask yourself, 'Why am I feeling anxious and why am I panicking?' Hopefully then you will find the answer the Universe is trying to teach you.

It's the same when we worry. We can't recognise that our worrying is causing us to panic and feel anxious. We worry about people, places, things, and situations we have no power or control over, and we do it time and time again without thinking about the consequences. It's insane really; you'd almost think we liked to panic and feel anxious, because we seem to do it on such a regular basis. But it's our old friend FEAR again, and it seems to be controlling our entire lives.

Fear is the root cause of all of our anxiety and panic attacks, and when we are worrying we are also causing problems within our bodies. When we panic, feel stressed or become anxious, it will start with an instant reaction... then our thinking takes over, and if we are in a habit of doing this it can be detrimental to our health and wellbeing. Heart disease, strokes, and heart attacks are common among those who worry a lot, get angry a lot, and panic a lot.

Any bad or sad news can cause us to panic and feel anxious; it's the way we have learned to react, so it's normal – and it hurts. Having to go somewhere or be around people can also cause many of us to panic and feel anxious. In earlier chapters we spoke a little about having no power or control over the past and future, in the same way that we have no power or control over others. So, when we are worrying about other people and things we have no control over, we lose our power.

Our power is our positive energy, and we keep this energy by accepting the things we cannot change. And when we learn to accept through awareness, understanding, and experience, we keep our power. Deep down, we know that worry will never solve anything, yet we continue to do it on a regular basis, and again we keep missing the lessons the Universe is trying to teach us. Time and time again we are shown these lessons, and time and time again we miss them. We miss them because we were taught to worry, so we see nothing wrong with it, when really, we should have been taught *not* to worry. Self-control means being in total control of oneself, and we do this by not interfering in things we already know we have no power or control over.

The difficulty in breaking this habit comes down to how you think you will feel about yourself when you finally do stop worrying. Some people feel that to worry is normal, so for them not to be worrying about other people and things seems absurd. Others worry about what others will think of them when they stop worrying, whilst some will be overwhelmed with gratitude and joy.

We have already experienced how it feels when we are not worrying, and we also know how it feels when we do worry. I know how difficult it is to break these chains of dysfunction, these horrid habits we have formed, and I know and understand how difficult change can be.

It's easy for me to say you have a choice, but it's not that simple, is it? Being aware you have a choice, along with the awareness and understanding you have, isn't enough to change anything. It takes action, determination, and courage, but you have these qualities within you and you have used them in the past. Seek and you shall find them again.

We are aware of the triggers as to why we panic, become anxious, and feel stressed, just as we are aware of the pain which comes from having these attacks. And although we want to stop having them, we have to realise that it takes time. We have to practise, my friends, but within weeks you will feel the difference as you learn to trust yourself more. Your body will always help you to become aware when your mind has reacted to something, and when we finally accept that we cannot change or control whatever it is we have reacted to, we keep our peace. And at the same time we can be proud of our progress.

There is always a trigger that causes a reaction, and that reaction is a habit, and that habit has caused us to panic and feel anxious. So, the only way for us to stop panicking and feeling anxious is to practise change. Once the trigger has been pulled and we are beginning to panic and feel anxious, we have to stop right away and check out our thinking. If we don't, those thoughts will take over and we will hurt.

This is when trusting ourselves comes in handy; we have to learn to trust ourselves so that we can change. We react, we panic, we become anxious, then tell ourselves lies that we can't cope and that something bad is going to happen, and before you know it we have a brown bag over our mouths to help us with our breathing.

It would help us if we were able to become more aware of our triggers. It would also help us with being truly upfront and honest with ourselves if we were to write down all the things that we believe have caused us to panic, feel stressed, and anxious over the years. And undoubtedly, when we look at all the people, things that have happened, situations we have been in, and the circumstances we have been faced with, we will find that we had no power or control over any of them. And the reason we had no power or control was because we gave it all away.

We lose our self-control as soon as we react in a negative way, and when we are being negative our power is drained because of what we are telling ourselves. Our batteries need charged because our positive energy is leaving our bodies, and when this happens we feel tired and weak. This is what fear does to us. It takes away all of our positive energy and any love we had for ourselves. We panic and become anxious and stressed before we get out of our beds in the morning because of what we are telling ourselves in our own heads.

That's why first thing in the morning is your most important part of the day, as we explained earlier. And I strongly suggest you try and remember the importance of first thing in the morning, especially if you have children!

I learned to prepare myself by reciting the Serenity prayer every morning and every time I was in a difficult situation. This helps to remind me of my powerlessness over other people, places, things, and situations. And when I accept that I have no power or control over people, places, things, situations, the past, and the future, I keep my power and my peace.

When I suffered from anxiety and panic attacks and wanted so much to be rid of them, I began to breathe in and out very slowly. Breathing in for 4 seconds, and breathing out for 4 seconds, and repeating this 3 times. And every time I did this, I came back to the present moment which is where the peace lies. Taking action is vital and our confidence grows, for we have ignited the spark which has awakened our spirit. When I found out about the breathing exercises and realised that they really helped with my anxiety, it prompted me to practise more – and that's what I did. I learned to meditate and breathe properly, and in doing so I slowed down my thinking, my breathing, and my life.

When we are aware of our triggers and we begin to understand why we panic and become anxious, we can begin to relax. With awareness and understanding, along with honesty and courage, peace is just around the corner and nothing can stop you.

By this stage in the book, you should be aware that fear is our enemy, and when there is fear in our lives, there's also panic, anxiety, and pain. We have no power or control over the past or the future, and every time we visit them we begin to panic, feel anxious, shameful, guilty, and regretful. So we really don't want to be going there!

Practise daily. Make it your job to be free from the expectations which are causing you to panic, feel stressed, and anxious – and the more you practise, the wiser you will become. There is no pain in the here and now, and that's why the present moment is a gift.

Live for the moment, be the moment. For the moment is the only thing that exists. It's when we leave the moment that the trouble begins and the fear and lies take over. Again, my friends, the process of change chapter will help you, so please don't panic!

## Forgiveness

Forgiveness is probably the most difficult lesson I came across on my journey. I personally found it difficult, due to my upbringing and the conscious and unconscious fears that were controlling me. Some people can forgive themselves and others at the drop of a hat – not many, but some can – whilst the rest of us just hold onto the shame, guilt, anger, blame, resentment, and fear, because that is all we know and understand.

Before we enter fully into this sensitive chapter, let's look at the meaning of forgiveness. According to the thesaurus, it is: absolution, charity, compassion, grace, mercy, reprieve, release, pardon, and respite. The opposites of forgiveness are accusation, blame, and punishment. This is what the thesaurus says forgiveness is and is not, but what it doesn't say is that forgiveness is a decision that has to come from the mind, the heart, and the soul.

We have to acknowledge all the hurt, pain, and wrongdoings, and then come to a decision to forgive ourselves and release these annoying lodgers who have been living in our heads rent-free. The ones we have judged, hated, resented, and condemned. And when we release the anger and bitterness we have towards the person/people and ourselves, we feel the pure, positive, loving and healing energy as the darkness is finally lifted.

When we forgive and show mercy to others, we also receive what we give. For what we give in life is what we get back, and if we live by these key spiritual principles, our spiritual wellbeing will flourish and blossom. Many people agree that forgiveness is needed for us to grow, even though it can be extremely difficult. It takes courage, but it also shows the true character and depth of the human spirit and how it can rise above past hurts and pain. True forgiveness and being able to let go of your past, with all its hurts, bitterness, anger, resentment, grudges, and pain, will bring healing to your mind, body, and spirit. True forgiveness is the key to inner peace and spiritual wellbeing. But how do we get there?

## Forgiving others

Sometimes you won't want to forgive, and that's understandable if the hurt went too deep, or because the person was too abusive, or expressed no regret. If you feel like this, my friends, please do not even attempt to forgive someone before you have understood, expressed, and released your anger and pain.

Forgiveness is a process, and if we work through the process, we will feel the difference. We all know how difficult and painful the process of recovery can be; whether it's a recent emotional injury or an older one, we can still carry the memories around with us. Deep down, we know we need to let go of all that anger and resentment, but it's extremely difficult when we don't know how. You might have even asked yourself at some point, 'How do I forgive?' then probably struggled for an answer.

Learning how to forgive is difficult, and it doesn't happen overnight. However, it is possible, and you'll be so much at peace that you'll wish you had done it earlier! Your body and your spirit will let you know when it is time to let go of someone/something, because we feel drained when we think of the person or people who have hurt us or whatever it was that happened. And it is these feelings of anger, resentment or hatred that prevent us from living our own lives.

Our spirit is crying out for us to change, as we are constantly living in the past rather than the present. We know that it is fear, hurt, pride or ego that has been holding us back from moving forward, but although we know this, some of us will use it to keep us safe from further hurt. Yet doing so also prevents us from receiving further joy and peace.

Try and remember the earlier chapters where we discussed the learned behaviours and habits we formed whilst growing up. For although we are responsible for our own thoughts, feelings, emotions, and lives, it is still difficult to forgive others who have hurt us due to the way we have learned to deal with our hurt.

Forgiveness is a personal thing, and sometimes we have to go deep within; no two individuals will experience it in the same way. But it's a vital process we have to go through in order for us to be free from the emotional pain we have carried with us. I had no happiness, poor health, and not an ounce of love whilst I carried hatred, anger, and resentment around with me, and I stayed trapped because I justified why I wouldn't forgive.

My life, my happiness, my health, and my relationships all paid the price for harbouring negative thoughts towards others. Then one day, I finally realised that I had hurt that time when they said what they said, and did what they did, and I was still hurting days, months, and even years later. And every time I thought about what they did or did not do, said or did not say, I hurt – badly at times – but the pain of carrying this heavy load was getting too much for me, so I had to learn to let go and forgive.

There are some things that people do and say that can cut us like a knife, and we will remember exactly what it was they said or did not say, what it was they did or did not do, and we hold onto this grudge/resentment, becoming hurt and angry every time we think about the incident. Yet there are other times when we get annoyed or angry at people but later forget about it. It's when we take things personally and hold a grudge that it hurts, and that's when we become ill.

Not reacting to negative people takes practice, and so does forgiveness. I can't tell you how to forgive, my friends; this has to come from the heart and soul. But if I can suggest four steps for you to follow, it may help:

**Step 1:** Use the awareness you now have, along with a true willingness to forgive. Again, your pain will help you here, but this time, instead of thinking about the other person/people and what they did or did not do, begin to look at your own life and see what this has done to you. For the only person who hurts through this is ourselves, and we have already experienced enough pain in our lives without carrying around someone else's darkness. Understanding where the other person is coming from and knowing that their behaviour has nothing to do with us, brings clarity. Try to understand that they are not reacting directly to us; they are reacting to their own thinking and their own insecurities. When you can finally see this, you will become less reactive and, instead of taking things personally, you can be grateful you are not in their shoes. Understanding and awareness are vital when it comes to forgiving others. Every act that comes from a place of unkindness is coming from a mind that is confused and a spirit which is dead. When others hurt us, it's because they are suffering themselves. Understanding this allows you to forgive, and gives you an opportunity to see the situation from a wider perspective – if you want to, that is.

**Step 2:** Surrender your right to get even. This is the heart of forgiveness! It's human nature to want to get even, because hurt people hurt people, and if this is what we have learned as we grew up, then this is what we will do. That's why we find forgiveness difficult at times. This is when the first step will come in handy, becoming aware of the length of time that you have carried this grudge/resentment around and the pain that it has caused within your life. If by any chance you are plotting revenge in some way, then that pain will never leave you; in fact, it will only get worse. Your pride and your ego will do its utmost to tempt you into taking revenge, and this is when your true character, awareness, and understanding must come into play. You have to remind yourself that we are spirit, and the reason we are here is so that we can learn to love, and we will never find true peace if we are harbouring resentment and plotting revenge. If you believe in karma, then you will know that what goes around comes around and that those of us who go against the laws of the spirit will have to pay that karmic debt. It's the same with society's laws. If you break them, you can go to prison, get fined, lose your home, and end up on the street. There are consequences to every thought and action in life. Knowing this and believing it helped me with the process of forgiveness and also to let go completely.

**Step 3:** Change from blame to understanding yourself. Whenever we are thinking about the wrongdoer and what they did or didn't do, we feel the distress within ourselves. The next time this happens, allow yourself to feel it; experience the experience without blaming the wrongdoer and without blaming yourself. Allow the experience to unfold, and then tell yourself that you are the master over your mind, body, and spirit, and no-one has the power to make you feel uneasy. Experience your emotions and embrace them; there's no need to chase them away, because it's important we focus on understanding ourselves and our emotions. By choosing to feel your emotions rather than blaming others for them, you learn to take responsibility and in doing so regain the power and control you gave away. Once this power and control is regained, you will see a bright new world with so much potential – and that's a promise.

**Step 4:** Healing and letting go – the final stage of forgiveness is letting go of your grudge/anger/resentment, and releasing those negative emotions from your body. Once we do that, we can actively move on with our lives. I once read that 'forgiveness is a gift you give primarily to yourself; it is more about you than the one you forgive.' And that is so true. Letting go of the past releases you from any ties you had with it. Try not to dwell over wrongs, otherwise you will be giving away your energy and you will stay tied to the past and the wrongdoer. Forgiveness helps to break this negative habit and gives you back the energy you have lost. It is a gift of freedom and healing for yourself, but also for the one you forgive. Being able to feel the feelings and being humble enough to forgive and let go is the most courageous thing a human can do. So be proud for being willing, be very proud. We may never understand why people hurt us, but that's ok. We don't have to know why something happened in order for us to get well and recover.

What's really important here that is you never blame yourself for anything or try to find excuses for the wrongdoer. Try, if you can, to take some time out to empathise with your wrongdoer for a moment. I know it's difficult, but it does help for us to see the reality of the situation at hand. Remember, we're human as well as spirit, we all make mistakes, we have all said and done things we are not proud of, and we all want to be forgiven.

When that day comes when you finally decide to forgive, be aware that you may still be tempted by the negativity, but you are free now to make choices and responses from a place of empowerment and not from a place of fear and anger. Remember also that this is a process and the ego is always out to get us, the obsessive chatterbox that wants to hold on and relive all of the negativity. If this happens and your ego wants to revisit the painful situation, ask yourself, 'Is this serving me because I have dealt with this?' Then tell yourself, 'I really do love myself now, and I know and trust that I really have forgiven, and I want only the best for me and for them.' Empower yourself, my friends, and then focus on the amazing life you deserve, because if you hold onto this pain you will never live.

I found this short example of unforgiveness within my papers one day. Unfortunately, I don't know who wrote it and I hope they don't mind me sharing it with you, but I loved it and feel it's appropriate for what we are talking about. See what you think:

> *UNFORGIVENESS – Being unforgiving is like being on a giant hook. Next to you on the hook is the person who has hurt you. The hook is extremely painful, and wherever you go, so does the hook and so does the offender. The only way you can get off the hook is if you allow the offender off first. The cost of not allowing the offender off the hook is, perhaps, a lifetime of unhappiness. Let go and live.*

## Forgiving ourselves

Now, if you thought that part was difficult, then wait until you read this part. This is the insanity of our minds, my friends. We can forgive others through time, but when it comes to forgiving ourselves we struggle, and we struggle badly. Why is that? Why can't we forgive ourselves for the mistakes we make, even though we have learned from some of them? I mentioned earlier that although we aren't doing the things we used to do, we can still feel the guilt and shame.

That's why this book is so important. We have to understand why we continue to do this to ourselves, for if we don't understand then we will continue to do it. I have worked with thousands of lovely people who have changed their thinking and behaviour but found forgiving themselves the most difficult. I have worked with thousands of people who have relapsed into old behaviours because they can't forgive themselves. Some have ended up taking their own lives.

One of the biggest obstacles I found in self-forgiveness was the tendency to wallow in our own guilt. We all feel bad because we know we've done wrong; everybody does that. But some of us actually draw those bad feelings towards ourselves like a magnet and refuse to stop the wailing. We might even try to use those bad feelings in order to justify our actions. We curl up in a ball, begin to feel sorry for ourselves, and sit on our pity pot, instead of taking responsibility for what we've done by trying to repair the damage or to make things right. And there are those who unconsciously decide to punish themselves by feeling miserable for the rest of their lives, like some kind of penance. Unfortunately, the decision to feel miserable for the rest of your life brings with it isolation and loneliness.

One thing for sure, my friends, misery loves company! And if you continue to punish yourself, then the person who is trying to love you will also feel as if they are being punished. It's a fact: anyone who's wallowing in guilt and self-pity is going to be less open than they normally would. They become more withdrawn, critical, and depressing, so whoever's around them – parents, partner, children, even animals! – is going to suffer.

Most of us find it difficult to forgive ourselves because of the way we have learned to think and behave towards ourselves. I read recently that studies on forgiveness have lead scientists to suspect that those who have difficulty forgiving are most likely to experience heart attacks, high blood pressure, depression, and other illnesses. There are so many different scenarios in life that can cause us to stay trapped within guilt and shame, and one of the biggest culprits is regret.

As you already know, I found it extremely difficult to forgive myself, due to my religious upbringing and the terrible fear I had of this God that had been instilled in me. No matter what it was, even the silliest of mistakes that most people would laugh at, I punished myself. And at times it was severe. I had lost my sense of humour, my self-confidence, and self-worth, due to this fear and I didn't know how to change it. All I kept saying was, 'I'm sorry.' I believed everything I had been told as a child, because I respected those who were teaching me, but what they taught me and the fear they instilled in me was wrong. And my own experience teaches me this. I couldn't forgive myself because I didn't deserve it, and the pain was my punishment. And I know there are millions out there who have had similar experiences. But as I mentioned earlier, we have nothing to fear now.

I truly understand the difficulty in self-forgiveness. For so many years we have been thinking the same way towards ourselves, so turning things around and being nice to ourselves is when it becomes difficult. We have lived so long with regret, shame, and guilt, and believed that it was okay to live like this, that it was 'normal'.

We all make mistakes and have accidents, but we find it extremely difficult to let go of some of them. Why on earth do we do this to ourselves? Because we have never known any other way. We find it hard to forgive ourselves because of the way we have learned to treat ourselves. For example, we use this horrible word 'failure'. And the negative power behind words like that can darken one's soul to the point where people have ended up taking their own lives.

We fail at nothing in life, my friends. We succeed in everything because we tried! And this word 'failure' and the feelings which come from thinking and believing you are a failure, will strip you of all your goodness. It's a lie. Our negative experiences in life are there to teach us valuable lessons, but we can't see that because we are not aware nor do we understand. You hear people saying my marriage/relationship has failed, and because they have chosen to use the word 'failed' many believe that they are also a failure and start to look for things to punish themselves.

We wing it as humans, as parents, husbands and wives, because we are not taught whilst growing up to build a relationship with ourselves first. A relationship based on getting to know and love oneself would help to prepare us for any relationship, marriage, and parenthood. But that would be too easy, wouldn't it? There would be no pain. We need to remember that no-one said this journey was going to be easy, but what they did say was that it would be worth it.

So, if we were to look back at our so-called 'failed' marriages/relationships through spiritual eyes and not society's, we would find that we never had a clue!. Did we learn from our first failure? Nope. Did we learn from our second, third, fourth failure? Nope. We just look at all these marriages and relationships as failures, punish ourselves severely, and tell ourselves we deserved it. But if we are honest, we simply didn't have a clue. We behaved the only way we knew how to behave, and tried our best with the tools we had at that time.

You're not a failure, my friends, and you should never punish yourself for not knowing or understanding anything about life.

This is a spiritual journey we are on, and the only way back to the innocence and the light is through experiencing the darkness and the pain. These are our lessons, and we can take them at any time when we choose to become responsible for our part. Were we passive and naïve or controlling and angry in our relationships? Were we co-dependent and full of fear of being alone? Were we dishonest, selfish, and inconsiderate? Or were we chasing this picture we spoke about earlier?

There are loads of questions and plenty of answers, but the reality is that we didn't know what we were doing was wrong. So, now that you know this, you can sort it, eh? Never allow your ego to tell you any different, and that's why we have to forgive ourselves. There's no book written or any law that I know of which says we should punish ourselves for the rest of our lives for the mistakes we make.

It's the same with people who are caught up in drugs, alcohol, gambling, sex, etc. They also find it extremely difficult to forgive themselves, and see themselves as total failures because of the things they did to feed their addictions – lying, cheating, stealing, manipulating, conning, etc. They forget that they were once innocent children who loved everyone and everything. If you ask any addict who is caught up in full blown addiction, they will tell you that they hate themselves and that they wish they were dead. They are not aware that it's the shame, guilt, anger, resentment, blame, and regret that they carry around with them that is keeping them trapped in their addiction. And until they learn this, they will always stay trapped.

Forgiving themselves is something they see as impossible because of the way their lives have turned out. But because of this way of thinking, most will relapse into old behaviours, and some will take their own lives because the guilt, shame, and regret is too much for them.

Our own thinking, my friends, our own negative thinking has taken us into addiction, and it's the same negative thinking which is preventing us from forgiving ourselves.

So, why can't we forgive ourselves? We can't forgive ourselves, because society says so. We are raised to believe that we should punish ourselves for the mistakes we make in life, rather than being taught to take the lessons from them. Yes, at times we can be selfish and inconsiderate, but did we know why we were behaving like that? Yes, our selfish behaviours can hurt others, and yes, we didn't do the things we said we would do, and at times we even meant to hurt others. But if you had the chance to rewind the clock, I'm pretty sure you would do things differently. Well, I'm hoping you would.

That's why it's so important that we learn from our mistakes, and Lorraine and I hope this book helps you to do that.

When you finally accept and admit that your behaviour has harmed someone, the process of change can begin. And when this moment comes around, the Universe will help you because you have finally admitted that you never knew that what you were doing was spiritually wrong. Admitting this takes courage, but so does forgiving yourself. But if you found the courage to admit your wrongs, then that same courage will help you to forgive, especially when you understand why you did what you did or didn't do. Sadly, if you justify, blame, or shift responsibility for your behaviour, then pain will always be your outcome.

Life is difficult, but being unwilling to forgive ourselves only makes it ten times worse. The best amends we can make to ourselves, family, friends, or anyone we have hurt, is for us to change our thinking and behaviour. No matter what it was you did or didn't do, punishing yourself for the rest of your life isn't going to change that.

I've made loads of mistakes, and I still have loads more to make. Some of these mistakes I never ever thought I would be able to forgive myself for, but I did. And so have thousands of others I have worked with, because we humbled ourselves and asked for help. I have worked with veterans who were raised Christian and with others who are non-religious, and both felt they could never forgive themselves for the innocent people and children who lost their lives through war. They held themselves responsible, and for years this had tormented them.

It's the same when I work with offenders and ex-offenders who have taken someone's life, either deliberately or not. None of these people ever thought it was possible to forgive themselves, but eventually they did. They wanted freedom, but felt they didn't deserve it. Yet through their willingness to understand, and by being humble enough and courageous enough to talk about it, feel it, accept it, and learn from it, they finally found the courage to let it go. All the people I have worked with showed true remorse for their past conduct, and that is why they found inner peace. Only we can truly forgive ourselves, my friends; no-one can do that for us.

You will never truly live unless you forgive yourself, so please stop punishing yourself, especially when you have felt the regret, shame and guilt, and shown remorse. You have paid the price, felt the pain, and have learned the lesson. Now it's time to be kind and loving towards yourself. The Universe will support and guide you through these changes, and you will experience beautiful feelings and emotions you only thought existed in books. Your confidence, self-worth, mental and physical health, as well as your personal relationships and circumstances, will all improve when you finally learn to forgive yourself.

## Let's recap:

Fear causes us to panic and feel anxious, as does living in the past and projecting into the future. And being unforgiving will always prevent us from being comfortable within our own skin.

This next chapter is very important, and Lorraine and I hope you will read it time and time again and enjoy doing so. Change is difficult but not hard, and the more you practise change, the more confident you will become. That's a promise!

# Chapter Nine

## Be transformed by a renewing of the mind

### The Process of Change

This section is all about change – and all it takes is courage, which you have already shown by getting this far into the book! Awareness and understanding is vital, which you already know from earlier chapters. Forgiveness, as we know, is the difficult one. But I know you have it within you, and hopefully through time you will find it within your heart, because it is truly the key to inner peace.

We also need a deep faith and a belief in ourselves that we can and will change; to never, ever doubt this belief; and, last but not least, to practise this daily.

That's right, daily practice. Like anything in life, if we don't practise it, we will never become good at it. Each day as you practise change, you will become more aware of the power within you, self-control and self-discipline will kick in, and you will become more aware of your own negative thoughts and reactions. But you will learn to control them, rather than allowing them to control you. It's like going back to school again! Except that this time you're learning about life and how to be responsible for this life.

Think about what I mentioned in an earlier chapter: we go to school for say 12 years (longer for some), then maybe to college or university for another two to seven years. Now, after all that learning and studying, we leave with… what? What did we learn about ourselves? Being educated won't remove your pain. But I can guarantee you that within a few weeks – not 15 years! – if you understand and practise what you are about to read, you will be walking on water.

So, before we start, do we agree that we didn't just wake up one morning as a negative, angry, depressive person riddled with fear, hurt, anger, shame, and guilt? Do we agree that we never came out of our mother's womb like that either? Do we agree that we have learned behaviours which are dysfunctional? And do we also agree that we cannot blame any more?

If you have agreed, great, you're ready. If not, then please continue anyway, as I know you will be ready soon. Being truly honest with ourselves can be difficult, as we now know, but you have nothing to fear now that you are beginning to understand.

I'm aware it takes courage, understanding, and a willingness to be free from pain before we can heal. But this is your time, my friends. You have these qualities within you, and hopefully you have taken something from what you have read so far, as this part is all about how to break these negative habits that you have read about.

Change is difficult, and don't let anyone tell you any different. If it was easy, the world would be free from pain. We can only hope that you have by this stage found the identification and understanding you longed for, and if you still have that willingness, then you will most definitely change.

This is why it takes courage, and hopefully you have found that through being honest and willing to face your fears. I'm also hoping that what you have read so far has helped you with the awareness and understanding around your fears; if not, go back and read it again and again until you know it off by heart.

If you want to be free from fear and pain, then you have to practise change and make it your job. I'm not asking you to write a 10,000 word essay or train for the Olympics, I'm only asking you to be mindful of the way you think, speak, and react. That's it; that's how simple it is. Don't tell me you find that confusing or complicated, do you?

It sounds so simple, doesn't it? Just those three things. But as you are now aware my friends, they are habits – and old habits are difficult to break.

## Being aware of our ego – the voice of lies

Change is a process, and it doesn't happen overnight. We have to learn to deal with our past, the skeletons in the cupboard, the things we did or didn't do that we still feel regretful, ashamed, and guilty about. The resentments and anger we have towards others, the lying and stealing, cheating, manipulating, bullying, racism, hatred, and fear. Then we have our own self-loathing, bringing ourselves down and belittling ourselves. These are all habits we really need to break, because we can easily form our own comfort zones within them.

All of these habits are formed by the way we think, the way we have learned to think. So, for us to change and break these negative habits and become spiritually well again, we have to learn to challenge our own thought process. When we begin to challenge and question our own thinking, our awareness becomes sky high. You have probably already begun to listen to your thoughts before you speak or act out on them, and this is you changing. You have hopefully now recognised that if you run with these thoughts, someone could get hurt... including you.

The ego, or chatterbox as I call it, is our most damaging habit and it is always out to get us. And, boy, is it powerful when we allow it in! It will always cause us pain and hinder our progress until we become aware of it. We have to remember that it's our own thinking which makes us feel good inside and bad inside, so try and look at your thoughts as energy. Positive thoughts and good deeds create positive energy and the feel-good factor; negative thoughts and selfish deeds create negative energy and the not-so-good factor.

That's why at times we feel drained and tired, and it's all down to that negative energy we are creating through our own negative thinking. Our bodies eventually break down to all this negativity, and as we get older we begin to visit our doctors more frequently and end up on all kinds of medication, because we weren't aware of our ego. All that negativity, fear, worry, anger, etc, has been eating away at our souls for years, and that's why we end up with pain throughout our bodies. 75% of the pain within our bodies comes through our thinking and behaviour!

You won't and don't see many positive thinking, healthy, shiny people at the doctor's. Oh no! They're too busy doing all that meditation, yoga, Tai-Chi stuff, out running and going to the gym, or walking up the hills with all their healthy drinks, smiling and laughing, confident and feeling good! And the reason they do this is because they're taking care of their mind, body, and spirit, and they are aware that they are responsible for it.

Some may have had previous problems with their physical and mental health, and others may have been given a second chance – a wake-up call, as we say. But one thing is for sure, the only difference between the addicted or depressed man or woman and the man and woman out running and looking healthy, is their thinking. No matter what our circumstances are, rich or poor, unemployed or in a job, happy or sad, it's how we think that makes us or breaks us. That's how simple we need to keep this.

No more blaming your past, or people from the past. This is your time, now you are ready, now you need to believe it. You have to learn to take action and become responsible for the way you think, and through daily practice you will be able to recognise your ego, the voice of lies. I am hoping you are more aware now and have a deeper understanding about life, but you also have to understand that our thoughts are very powerful and our ego is always out to get us.

For example, before we have even opened our eyes in the morning, that little voice appears. My grandmother, bless her, always used to say to me, 'Gerard, prepare yourself well in the mornings, son, as this is when the devil is at your bedside doing press-ups, waiting on you getting up!' It took me years to understand what she meant, but now I truly understand it as I've experienced it.

This same little voice knows where to get us; it plays on our weaknesses and tempts us continuously. This same little voice is the one which tells us to stay in bed a little longer so we can sleep in, and then panic because we know we are going to get into trouble and maybe lose our jobs. The same voice – 'our own thoughts, remember?' – tells us, 'I'm not well. I can't be bothered getting up today. I'm depressed. I can't be bothered seeing anyone today. I'm fed up. I don't want to be here. What's the point?'

The next minute, the duvet cover is over your head and you don't seem to see anything wrong with that! Fair enough, some of us might have had some sad news or broken up in a relationship, so it's understandable to want to hide away. But for most people within society, it's because they listen to their ego and believe the lies that it is telling them. And that is before you have even opened your eyes or got out of your bed!

How often do we start our days off with negativity and dread going to school, college, university, work, etc, and we never do anything about it. This is something we really need to change, because we know now that this little voice will stay with us all day if we allow it, and the next day, and the next, etc.

As we have identified that change is a process, we have to become aware of what it is we need to change before that process can begin. I know it sounds like we need to change hundreds of different things here, but believe me, once we change how we think and the way we react to our own thinking, everything else fits into place. Our ego is powerful, and I will share with you just how powerful it is. It's our own thinking we are addicted to, and it's our own thinking which dictates the course of our lives. From first thing in the morning until last thing at night, this little voice is living in our heads rent-free. It tells us what to do, where to go, what to say, how we feel. And like sheep, we just run with these thoughts and do as we are told, because we believe that what we are thinking is normal.

That same little voice is also the one that tells you that you are better than others – and a lot of people really believe this. Thinking we are better than others and being over-confident and cocky is the ego at its best. We are all equal, my friends, and we have all had the pleasure and experience of watching how the high and mighty can fall because of their inflated egos. Abusing the power you have over others and believing you are superior over others, goes against your true self, and listening to your ego in this way will only bring pain and loneliness. At first, we think nothing of it, but as the saying goes, 'Karma is a bitch!'

They say that karma means that whatever we give in life is what we will get back; what we sow, we will reap; what goes around, comes around. That's all true, but we also need to remember that our own thoughts create our own karma, and if we are thinking the same thoughts on a daily basis, then we are going to feel the same way on a daily basis. As you think, so shall you feel?

It's simply all down to our thinking. One thought leads to another, then another, and so on. For example, if your first thought when you awaken in the morning is, 'I need a fix, or a drink', then that's what you will believe. You really believe that is what you need to get you by. It's the same with any of society's addictions, they all begin with a thought. And if you are thinking the same way every day, then this is what you will experience each day. You listen to the thought then you act on it, and this is why you stay trapped within your own thoughts. And unless you change the way that you think, then you will continue to stay trapped within your own thoughts.

That's why change takes courage; that's why we have to be aware of our ego and the pain which comes from the lies we have learned to tell ourselves. We are not bad people, we are not weak; we are strong, loving, caring people who find life and its challenges and obstacles difficult to handle. We all find life difficult to deal with, because we didn't know any better and nobody ever told us any different, so we just went with the norm. But as we now know, my friends, it's not normal to tell yourself you are a bad person all the time because you make mistakes or other people call you bad, and it's not normal to loathe and criticise yourself, judge and condemn yourself, and continuously bring yourself down.

Do you see that as a normal healthy way to think? I mentioned earlier that if someone was to speak to us in the street in the same way as we speak to ourselves in our own heads, what would we say or do to them? No, you wouldn't laugh. You would probably punch them, or give them a mouthful back. Insane, isn't it? It's totally crazy the way we treat ourselves – and all because of our good friend, the ego.

The ego will prevent you from changing, and it will also prevent you from loving. I could write what I have read about love to impress you and make myself out to be someone I'm not, but I won't do that. That's an old behaviour! But what I will do is share my definition of love with you, and that is simply to be absent of all negative thoughts towards myself and others, to always see the good in myself and others. In doing this, I feel what I presume to be love. Again, I had to ask myself, 'Can I do this? Can I really feel love?' My answer was 'Yes', and why not? Why can't we see the good within ourselves and others?

We have all experienced how our ego can get us into trouble; we spoke about it in the learned behaviours' chapter. How we can easily find ourselves gossiping, judging, and criticising other people and thinking it's alright at the time, and completely forgetting that we ourselves detest other people who judge, criticise us and gossip about us. So, why do we do it when we know deep down that it's wrong? It's that little voice that wants to get us into trouble and cause us to hurt and hurt badly. Our ego prevents us from seeing the truth, and that's why we always have this battle going on inside our heads. It's like the wee devil on one shoulder and the wee angel on the other shoulder. The wee devil is your ego and the wee angel is your conscience, and your health and wellbeing depends on which one you listen to.

When we are feeling uncomfortable within, it's down to us listening to our ego. Think about the many times you have had an argument with yourself, or you're walking along the road ranting and raving about someone or something. Do you ever question yourself who it is you are arguing with and talking to? You're talking to your ego, my friends, and we all do it nearly every day. We see people walking through the city getting angry and annoyed with themselves and talking out loud, and we laugh at them. And the funny thing is that we really do believe this to be normal.

Being true to yourself and being totally aware of your ego is paramount for your continuous growth. Our ego can put us in some very dangerous situations because of the lies it tells us and the false evidence it helps us to gather within our minds. So, before we can change and really learn to be confident again, to be loving and happy, we have to be aware of our ego, the voice of lies.

To explain the ego in simple layman's terms, I would use the snake in the Adam and Eve story in the Bible. Now, whether you believe in the story doesn't matter, but what's important is the spiritual message the story tells us. Adam and Eve were innocent, just like us, and they walked about the Garden of Eden naked just like we did within our own homes. They were loved by their creator, happy and grateful as they had everything they could possibly need within the garden, just as we had as children within our homes. Their creator loved them so much that He promised them everything within the garden – and I mean everything – apart from one thing. He was spoiling them in the same way as we are all spoiled as children. As we know from the story, that one thing they were asked not to touch was a certain tree; they could eat as much fruit as they wanted from all the other trees, but they were not to touch the fruit from this particular tree because it was dangerous. Sound familiar, folks? As children, we are also warned of the dangers by our creators, but do we listen?

After explaining the dangers, He left them to play in the beautiful garden. As Adam and Eve were still innocent and naked at this time, they continued to play in the beautiful garden with all the beautiful flowers, trees, and fruit. Then all of a sudden and out of nowhere, this snake appears beside the tree they were warned not to touch. Because they were innocent, like children, they had no fear, but they had never seen a snake before so they were curious and went over to the tree to investigate. And that's when the trouble began.

The snake began to whisper in Eve's ear, tempting her that she could become as great as her creator, even greater, and all she had to do to achieve this was to take a bite of the apple from the forbidden tree. Now, the snake was very cunning. It was lying to Eve, and its whole purpose was to hurt them both and get them thrown out of the garden, so it continued to continuously tempt poor Eve.

The snake was telling Eve that her creator was bad and that He didn't want them to eat the fruit from this tree as it contained amazing powers, and if Adam and Eve were to eat this fruit then they would become greater than their creator which was the reason He had forbidden them from eating from it. And the snake wouldn't shut up. It continued to tempt our Eve, until she finally gave in and took a bite from the apple. As soon as she took her bite, she shouted Adam over to take a bite as well.

Adam knew, just like Eve, that they were not to eat the fruit from this tree, but – just like us – the temptation was too much and he sought Eve's approval, so he also took a bite from the apple. Of course, as soon as they ate the apple, they lost their innocence, and guilt and shame appeared within them for the first time. They covered up their nakedness or private parts with fig leaves and ran away and hid in the garden as they were so frightened and ashamed. And we do exactly the same when we know we have done wrong.

When their creator came looking for them, He knew they had done something wrong because they were hiding from Him and they had covered themselves up. This hurt their creator as He had given them everything they ever needed, but it wasn't good enough for them and they wanted more. And that's what we do as children, my friends, we forget our gratitude.

Our parents also knew when we had misbehaved as it was written all over our faces and we tried to hide it by either covering it up, running away, or blaming – very similar to Adam and Eve, wouldn't you say?

Now their creator was so angry with them for being disobedient that He put them out of the beautiful garden which had everything in it that they could ever want. They were now out on the street, as we would say, with no love or guidance from their creator. They now had to fend for themselves and find somewhere warm to stay, to find food and clothes, and to learn about life because they had lost their innocence. And if you have read the story of Adam and Eve, then you will know that due to them yielding to the temptation with the snake and being disobedient, they not only lost their innocence but they lost their guide and creator, their home which was paradise, and became absent from the source of love as they were now living in fear.

They'd had everything they could ever imagine, but chose to listen to the temptation, 'the ego', and in doing so they ended up living a life of dysfunction. And when their children were born, they learned from their parents, and Cain killed his own brother, Abel. And the story of life continues to this present day.

The snake is our ego, my friends, and the Adam and Eve story explains what can happen to us when we listen to this snake. We might not see it but we can hear its whispers, and we know now what to expect if we listen to its temptation. The ego is the dark side of life, and when we listen to it, it brings nothing but pain. Our conscience is our spirit, the light and our guide, and when we listen to it and are obedient to it, we feel nothing but love.

## Awareness and recognition

Now's the time where you have to ask yourself, am I ready? For us to change, we first have to recognise our ego and the negative thoughts which cause us to react the way we do and, believe me, they can dress themselves up and sneak in at any time. So this is where your awareness, honesty, and determination come in handy.

You will be able to recognise when the negativity enters, as our bodies always warn us. As soon as you feel the discomfort within you, that's the sign that your thinking has changed. How do you know this? Simple. When we think good, we feel good; when we think bad, we feel bad. Remember the reactions part of the book, and the things which cause us to react: what we see, what we hear from others, and what we tell ourselves. This awareness is the pearl within your oyster. Use it wisely and your future is destined for great things. Recognising and becoming aware of the negative thoughts through the shift within your body, is the beginning of change. It's a warning sign you need to be grateful for.

Our own thoughts set off this reaction – what we have seen, heard, or told ourselves sets the chain in motion. And for us to change, we have to become more responsible for the way we react to these negative thoughts. Fear nothing, as fear is only an expectation; try and remember that!

And don't fear what others will think of you when you choose this new path. This is when you will find out who your true friends are. As we discussed earlier in the book, our own parents and members of our own family can become jealous of us, but if we allow this to get to us, it will hinder our progress. Also remember: this is about *you* changing; we can't change other people! We are powerless over others and how they think and behave, and that's why it's useful to read back over some of the previous chapters now and again. Knowing this and accepting this is growth, and growth brings on change, and with these changes other gifts come along.

This, however, is where change becomes difficult! Now we are aware and understand that we alone are responsible for how we feel at this moment in time, and every moment thereafter. And the way we *feel* at this present moment is down to the way we are *thinking* or *not thinking* at this present moment. We only have this moment, and each moment is precious when we live within it. You have read and experienced the pain which comes from living in the past and future – they are two places we have no control or power over, and every time we visit them, we get hurt badly.

As you're reading this, you're in the moment, which is where the peace lies – and I hope you're enjoying it! But if we leave this moment and we allow our minds to take us into the past or future, we are in trouble, especially if we have negative thoughts.

We have to learn to use our past as our greatest asset in order to learn from our past mistakes. This is how we learned to be honest at the beginning, so that we could learn from our mistakes and help others along the way. Entering into the future in a positive way, with confidence, gratitude, and a true belief about what you want to do in life, is great. And it will happen because it's going to help you grow as a person, once you get rid of your ego! Going into the past in a negative way will always cause regret within our lives, unless we deal with it, learn from it, embrace it, and share it if you truly believe it can help others.

Entering into the future in a negative way will always cause anxiety and fear, because we are not accepting that we have no power or control over it. Also, we begin to gather false evidence and behave as if we were God, thinking that we know what the future holds.

But within this precious moment, there lies peace, and we always have that choice. That's why we need to practise being aware of our thoughts and where they can take us, and we will be able to do that by becoming aware of the shift within our bodies.

The shift in the body I'm talking about is when one minute we are feeling comfortable in ourselves, and the next minute we are feeling uncomfortable. Change is about recognising these triggers and understanding that the shift occurs through sight (things that we see); sound (what we hear from others); and what we tell ourselves in our own heads. Our job is to try and become aware of these negative thoughts within the moment, and learn to take responsibility for them through recognising the shift within our bodies. That shift is the warning sign.

I know it's difficult, my friends, but with practice you will master it. You will be able to catch the thought before you run with it. You might even run with it for a sentence or two and then catch it, or you might run into a few paragraphs of negativity before you catch it. But whatever you do, please try and catch it before it runs into a book, otherwise your whole day will be filled with negativity.

When we allow our ego head-room, it takes over and ends up ruining our days and our lives. When we finally recognise and catch the thoughts which bring us down, we are also breaking the old habits – and this is tremendous progress.

## Catching and challenging the thought

You were probably wondering what I meant when I said 'catch and challenge the thought'. This comes through awareness and practice, as the previous paragraphs have explained, but also through recognition, the shift and the feeling within our bodies and stomachs. Please believe me, if you look at this as a challenge and you feel you are up for it, then I can promise you without any doubt whatsoever that you will feel joy, peace, and serenity very soon. You will be confident in all that you do because you are aware of the thoughts which previously took your confidence away. You will live and experience all your dreams and more because you are now aware that you are in control of your own life and destiny. Your health will improve, your circumstances and personal relationships will change, and you will find true happiness.

You have already read what happens to us when we chase and search for things to make us happy. Instead, be truly grateful for what you have, and more will be given. For when we are grateful and responsible for the money we have, and learn to live by our needs and not our wants, life becomes so much easier.

You are already aware that the way we think and behave at times can cause us to hurt. We also know that the way we think and behave towards others can cause harm. So, keeping this simple: for us to change, we need a little humility. Humility will destroy your ego and pride, and will help you immensely on your new path. If someone thinks that they are right and you believe them to be wrong, then... let it be. It's not important any more.

Arguing over who's right and wrong is just our egos clashing; humility destroys the ego by allowing the other person to believe that they are right even though they might be wrong. We need to catch ourselves when we are in this type of situation. For the only way for us to measure our progress and our complacency is when we are faced with hostility, confrontation, and other situations we previously reacted to in a fearful, controlling, aggressive, or passive way.

A true desire to be free from your old life and the pain which came from it should be enough motivation for you to say, 'I've got this. I can do this.' To ask yourself, 'What am I doing? Why am I thinking this way? Why am I doing this?' is you challenging yourself. And when we question our pattern of thought, we are then becoming aware of it and its motives; we are catching it before it festers and reaches our stomachs.

For example, if we see and hear something that we don't like, we will react the way we have always reacted. For us to change that negative reaction or response, we have to change how we see ourselves, see others, and see the situation. We do this through our new understanding, awareness, and the practice of humility. When we are free from fear, we will react with empathy and love, and our thoughts will always be positive, for that's who we are.

This is a choice we all have, my friends. We can continue to allow our ego to control us, or we can learn to control it. Deep down, we know it's wrong to think negatively towards ourselves and others, as it only causes pain. Challenge your old ways of thinking, and do it gently. Never be angry, as the ego wins on both counts then. Always be kind, and gentle, and proud, when you catch it.

Once you have decided you are going to do this, through practice you will be able to catch the negative thought; that's a promise. Your awareness and recognition will help you to catch the thought before you run with it. Catching the thought and challenging yourself on the spot is you empowering yourself and working towards being the master over your own mind.

No matter what you did in the past, you have to learn to forgive yourself before you can move forward. You have the courage, awareness, and understanding, now it's up to you to believe you can change.

Words and thoughts, my friends, that's all they are; good energy and bad energy. So, try your best to always create good energy by having good thoughts, and if you practise on a daily basis to catch yourself when your mind wanders, you will find that inner peace I promised you by living in the moment. Nobody likes change, but this is your life – and we only get this one chance.

This book was written for you, my friends. Change is difficult, but with the awareness and understanding you have now, anything is possible – and I mean anything.

## Remember:

When your day begins, prepare yourself by focusing on the here and now, the present moment.

Begin your day as you mean to end your day, for you are now in control.

Be aware of what it is you have to do that day, and then leave it at that. We have to learn to trust ourselves that we will remember what it is we have to do; if not, then keep a diary.

Keep things as simple as you can, and you will be able to catch yourself when you are thinking ahead of yourself.

We don't have to talk to ourselves all day. Remember, we only have a moment, and when we live within that moment we will be able to catch the negative thought. But if our mind is yapping away at a hundred miles an hour, then we will never catch the thought or find peace.

Catch it, challenge yourself, then let it go; catch it, challenge yourself, then let it go. Practise this daily, and you will master it.

# Chapter Ten

## Final thoughts

Well, that's the story of life in simple layman's terms, my friends, and the process that we need to go through for us to change and find peace. A life without fear and worry lies within us, and all we have to do is to change how we see ourselves, others, and the world.

I'm not asking you to do something I haven't done myself. I'm well aware of the difficulties and fears you have to face before you can change, but I didn't know then what I know now – and that's the reason for this book. I didn't know how to change; my own pain motivated me to get to where I am today, and I'm hoping it's the same for you.

Hopefully, you have the awareness and understanding about life now, so that you can learn to practise change without going round in circles blaming, searching, and hurting as I did and many, many others did before me.

We have tried to present the information in these chapters in a very simple way, and without any jargon, because the messages we are trying to get across to you are simple and straightforward.

We now know that we didn't just wake up insecure, and we know life can be very tough and cruel at times. But when we realise what life's about, and learn to understand and accept ourselves, we will experience life and its purpose.

Here are some crucial facts worth remembering:

✦ We were all innocent children once.

✦ We unconsciously copied what we saw and heard as children growing up within our homes and living environments.

✦ The way we think and behave has also been learned over a period of time.

✦ The negative way we can react to certain people, places, things, and situations is also a learned behaviour.

✦ All these negative behaviours and ways of thinking are habits, and these habits are the cause of all our unhappiness and pain.

You are also now aware that you have a choice each and every morning about how you start your day, and that is why Lorraine and I have given you a new set of tools to help you to break these old habits and finally be rid of all this negative energy so many of us are carrying around. The tools which lie within us all are honesty, courage, awareness, understanding, empathy, gratitude, and love. And if you use these tools every day, then nothing can tempt you, because you are now living within the moment.

It's always good to remember that temptation will always be there, but never forget that any temptation is only a thought. And our awareness has taught us not to run with any negative thoughts, but to catch them and to challenge them. I can promise you that when you practise this and begin to catch these thoughts, your self-control and self-discipline will go through the roof, and soon you will not need to challenge and catch these negative thoughts any more. You will eventually just allow the negative thoughts and temptation to pass you by, as you become aware that you alone are in control.

I never in a million years thought I could change and find peace within my life. I thought life was just about pain. But as you have read, life's about being honest with ourselves that we know nothing about life. All we knew about our lives is what we learned from others, and the things we learned confused us and caused many a complication.

Your mistakes, your pain, your laughter, your joy, your own experience and future experiences are your only teachers now.

Learn from your past, don't stay trapped in it.

You now know that pain comes from within us because of the way we are thinking and behaving towards ourselves and others.

We are also aware that we can always feel good when we are thinking good and doing good.

You know that you are spirit, and when you are thinking positively, being grateful, having kind, loving thoughts, and showing love and compassion, you feel really good inside.

And when we are being selfish, inconsiderate, disrespectful, disloyal, ignorant, angry, resentful, and frightened, we feel the complete opposite.

We all have choices. The benefit of thinking positively and doing positive things is that you will never have to feel fear, shame, guilt, anger, resentment or worry ever again. I promise you will enjoy your new life as you are beginning to understand who you are now and why you are here.

Hear no evil, see no evil, and speak no evil. Remember the three wise monkeys? Use it as a mantra each morning or begin with a gratitude list, this will always lift your spirit in the morning.

You could begin your list with: 'I am grateful that I have a roof over my head and a bed to sleep in; a partner or spouse to wake up with when others have nobody; I am grateful for my children, family and friends; food in the cupboards and money in my pocket, no matter how much it is, especially when there are others worse off than me; I'm grateful for my eyes that I can see, ears that I can hear things, and a tongue that I can speak with; I am grateful for my arms, limbs, and senses, the air that I breathe; and the beautiful people and things I get to see; And most of all, I am grateful for the lessons you show me each day.'

Believe me, gratitude is probably the most important virtue to possess, for with gratitude all good things come to you. No pain or darkness can ever get near you because you are attracting all the positive energy and love through being grateful for what you have. Hopefully you are aware now that when you look at what you haven't got, you will always be in pain. Knowing this will set you free to enjoy the rest of your journey and your life.

Keep trusting in yourself, and never doubt yourself. Never, ever quit or give up. This is your time, take it, be grateful for it, and embrace it.

The power lies within us, my friends. You are aware of this now, and you realise that the truth will set you free from the lies you have been telling yourself for years. Tell yourself, 'I am courage; I am strong; I am loving and kind; I am truly grateful.' And believe it, because it is the truth.

The only thing that will prevent you from changing is fear, and now that you understand what fear really is, there is nothing that can stop you. Detaching from negative influences – including family and friends – will be difficult at first, but please remember that their behaviour is bringing you down and causing you to feel pain at times, and if you continue to be around them, then you will continue to be in pain.

This is *your* life, *your* journey, and *you* are the one who wants to change, they are not. Never forget that; you are totally powerless over others. Don't allow anyone or anything to stand in your way, for you now have the courage, the awareness and understanding, and with these new tools, you are well on your way.

You could maybe try and find a new hobby or interest, like yoga, Tai-Chi, or a meditation group, where you will be around like-minded people who are all trying to stay healthy within mind, body, and spirit. Actions speak louder than words, and the more action we take, the better the result; the more we practise, the more confident we become. Slow down and enjoy the changes – there's no rush to die! We all have loads to learn, so embrace your new beginnings and keep trusting yourself.

Once you learn to keep the focus on you, instead of others, you will experience the peace we have written about. And once you learn to quiet your mind, you will experience and understand the true meaning of serenity.

As I mentioned several times, we are never alone on our spiritual journey and when we connect with our source of life, our creator, we experience guidance and support, as well as healing, wisdom, and unconditional love.

This is what we are entitled to, so ask and you shall receive. And as soon as you decide to change, the Universe will know and it will set things in motion for you.

One word of caution. Please try and remember that certain things we ask for in life take time to materialise, so be patient and try not to doubt yourself or the process. Also try and remember, my friends, that we knew nothing but thought we knew everything, and that's why we ended up in pain.

Lorraine and I hope and pray that what you have read within the book will help you to get to know yourself, your true self, and when you experience this, you will also experience the power which lies within us. And that power, my friends, is unconditional love. May you find it now.

## About the Authors - Gerard Murphy

For over 30 years I searched for happiness in other people, material things, money, drugs and alcohol and saw nothing wrong with that, everyone else did but I couldn't see it. I really thought it was normal to think, behave and react the way I did. I lived my life in total fear and couldn't see that either . Mental institutions, drug and alcohol clinics and hospitals and still I continued to blame as I never had a clue what was happening to me. Even when I began to change my life around I was still living with fear, anger, guilt, shame and regret. Living with these thoughts and behaviours, feelings and emotions and seeing nothing wrong with them kept me trapped in pain for a very long time. I wasn't aware, nor did I understand anything about myself or life but thought I knew everything. Learning to read and write at 35 was difficult but changing how I think, how I react to my thinking and how I react to other people, well, that's probably the greatest challenge I have ever taken on. I found change extremely difficult, not hard, but difficult and that's why I wrote the book. When I began to get honest I finally realised that I alone was responsible for my own thoughts, my own feelings, emotions and most importantly, my own life. Once I became aware of this and began to understand what happened to me and why I behave, think, feel and react the way I do, I could then begin the process of change. In making these changes I chose to share these experiences with others in order that the cycle of dysfunction can be broken within their lives. I knew with awareness and understanding and a little gratitude they would find joy and become powerful examples to their children, family, friends and anyone who needs guidance.

**Contact**

lifeinlaymansterms@gmail.com

https://www.facebook.com/gerard.murphy.5245

## About the Authors - Lorraine Buchanan

I am 55-year-old mother of 2 and grand-mother of one, I lost my husband Ian to alcoholism in 2001. For 7 years prior to his death I watched him battle to sustain sobriety and always relapsing no matter what services he was attending. I couldn't understand why these services or the services I approached weren't able to help with the causes of relapse. After living in what can only be described as a living hell and losing Ian, I swore his death would not be in vain. If I could see what would bring him peace, I could show other people, this led to writing "The Power of Example". People reading it thought it was written for them or about them. Some of them asked for a group which started and led to a drop-in service, where it was apparent people needed to understand what happened to them and why they were responsible for their own thoughts and behaviours. We then wrote, and developed programme called "Empowering by example" after identifying thinking and behaving patterns which prevented the healing process. I still work with people helping them to become resilient to the challenges they face and achieve a sense of well being.

Printed in June 2022
by Rotomail Italia S.p.A., Vignate (MI) - Italy